The Sum of Everything

Book 2

Also by Ahmi Beppu

The Sum of Everything, Book 1

The Sum of Everything

The Human Existence in Relation to Heaven

Book 2

Ahmi Beppu

First paperback edition, January 2019

ISBN 978-0578444482

Library of Congress Control Number: 2019900249

Contents

Prologue III

This World is Our Dream 1

Decision Making 8

Birth and Death 14

The Mirror of Life 23

Where the World Stops and Begins 28

Fate 40

To Forgive but Not Forget 44

The Secret of Attraction 48

The Elemental Table 54

The Lark 60

The Ego 66

What We Know of Being 75

There Comes a Day 83

How to Change the World 86

Paris 97

Once Upon a Life 100

Lost and Found 105

The Mirror That is Mental Illness 109

The Blank Script 117

What's Duke's Kind of Holiday 123

The Plague That Never Ends 131

The Four Seasons 135

Goodnight Moon 140

The Answers You Seek 141

O'er the Land and Seas 145

Manifesto to Myself 148

Manifesto to My Children 150

The Sins of My Fellow Man 152

A Poem 155

The Deceptive Mind 158

Good Night, My Sweet 160

Don't Doubt, My Friend 162

Personal Trauma 164

Why Are We All Afraid to Experience Joy? 169

Energy Expressed 172

Awareness is Key 177

What is Happening Right Now 185

You Think You Have Loved 192

Soul Mates 206

There is No Big Secret 208

The Investigation Into the Self 218

The Investigation into the Self II 226

Fear 228

Zenmaticism 236

A Tale to Heighten Your Senses Part 2 242

Pony 250

What Have You Given to Your Fellow Man? 253

The Root of All Suffering 259

Can We See the Truth in the False 263

The Sum of Everything 267

For

My Beloved, My Twin Flame,

Through your eyes I fell in love with myself. You opened me up to an experience I didn't think was possible. You led me over the rainbow to my heaven on earth. In this I awakened to the truth that this wasn't something I found outside myself but was always within me.

Prologue

Many questions have probably arisen from reading the first book in this series, The Sum of Everything. Things of this nature aren't always so easy to understand, and it may take time to process what is revealed to you. My hope is that you read the first book with an open mind and read it more than once. As you re-read the words you will find different meanings and understanding. You may find different emotions inside yourself or answers you didn't find the first time you read it. If you are searching for an answer, open the book and so shall you be given the answers you seek.

In this book, we'll dive deeper into your awakening so you can discover answers based on your own truth, your own will. Your will is your ultimate power. The words expressed here are not to control or deceive your free will. They are meant to help open your awareness and expand your perspective if you so choose. You hold the reins in life. You are the only one that makes choices or decisions for yourself. You decide how to react, how to feel and how to think. How you view life is out of your own free will. Anything or anyone who tells you otherwise is sorely deceived.

Your free will has led you to pick up this book. Something inside you—whether consciously or not—is open and ready to explore the nature of your existence. Your power. Your true self. You listened to the call and here we are now at the start of our time together. Thank you for being here.

As you read this text, I ask you to come together with higher energies. Let us join as one on the same level. As we talk, discuss, ponder and express together we can find a place of trust and truce. The only way to create this free communication is to release all that we know of life, love, heaven, earth and ourselves. When we shed our physical skins, we are our naked true self. At this level, there is nothing to differentiate us. We drop our race, our gender, our cultures, our religions, our beliefs, our traditions and our "truths." There is no one here telling you what to do, how to think and what to believe. We are communicating, opening our awareness to endless possibilities. We don't find fact or fiction in our discussions. We don't say yes or no. We are sharing our awareness, finding who we really are.

The point of this book is four-fold: to open your awareness; to unearth the impossible; to find your individual truth through experience; and to open the pure love inside yourself. Ultimately, to transform your reality into your heaven on earth. Truth comes through experience. Most cannot find truth in something they have not experienced. The human mind wants proof. It wants to see it and feel it firsthand. The words in this book are not meant to give you someone else's truth. The goal is to help you open your awareness, to help guide you to find your own truth through your own experience. Not someone else's. Truth as heaven defines it is just your ultimate happiness, peace, love and harmony. Any other idea of truth is false. If someone's idea of "truth" brings hardship, frustration, suffering, pain and, above all, fear, it is not truth. Love is the ultimate truth. Anything that is not aligned with love is not truth. To think otherwise is a deception of the mind due to the false reality that is the physical or the world, as you know it.

As you read we can come together to delight in each other, to share in each other's perfection and give light and love to others who may find this book in their hands.

Books fall into our hands at the perfect time. There is always guidance, answers to our pondering minds and things we need to know. As you read this book see it as just that. There was a reason you found yourself here with this book. There is a reason for everything.

This World is Our Dream

This world is our dream. It is our creation. We hold the power to have, to be, to create this illusion. Isn't life but an illusion, a dream, fleeting moment to moment? Everything around us is there solely to create our fantasy. The people around you, the noise, the conversation, the experience, everything is there for you, a creation chosen by you. You must become aware of this. This is when the delusion of the illusion occurs. A delusion of the illusion is to find truth in something that is false. The physical is the illusion, which, for the most part, is already the false; the delusion is accepting the illusion. You are deceiving your mind into seeing something that is not really there. That is being delusional. We label it as a mental illness. It is only when it gets out of hand and causes extreme hardship to someone's daily functions that we label them as delusional.

Most mental illness stems from a delusional mental state. As a whole don't we all live in a delusional state? We all see the false in the false. We never really see the truth. Every aspect of life is an illusion. It is being aware of this that frees us of the effect it has. That is when the mind is truly free. We all see something or experience something and label it as the truth. That is true because I saw and heard it. The truth shall set you free and it really will. When you can find the truth behind everything in every moment you will see how false reality is. This may scare you at first. You may feel a lack of security because it is holding on to the false that gives us a sense of security. The human mind usually deceives us into only believing that what we physically can see is secure. When you hold on to that false security, you hold on to the things that are fleeting and insecure. So when you lose that sense of security or that thing that gives you security it causes you an extreme amount of suffering and hardship. The suffering is due to the conflict in your mind. The idea that nothing is secure creates great duress because your sanity and your existence are maintained by your sense of attachments to these falsities. People's fears are so great. All of this fear you tie to yourself, to other people, to things, to experiences, to situations. Your mind thinks the only happiness you have is tied to these things. Without certain people or things, you feel empty, unfulfilled and possibly unhappy. This goes to such an extent that it brings about so much fear that you feel this is an attack on your life. That you cannot live without this "thing" that is your security. This then causes depression, anxieties, disease, physical pain and other mental dysfunctions. Usually, these "things" that you tie yourself to are not truly giving you the happiness or fulfillment that you think they are. When you are in a state of anxiety you are not happy, you're not fulfilled and therefore you are unable to give and receive pure love. Pure love can only flow in a state of open channels. Fear is an energy wall that stops the flow of love and light energy. Where there is darkness there cannot be light. All you are able to give is that fear (aka anxiety) for that is what fuels your every action, decision and thought. Release the fear to allow the light into your darkness. What have we learned in our awareness? We have learned that we cannot receive something that we are not. To find pure love we must first find it within our self. It is the energy we give that creates our reality. Our energy we are giving out is constantly manifesting what is in our outer world. What relationships and experiences you attract are the result of the energy you're expressing through your thoughts, words and actions.

Energy never stops flowing. Without energy, nothing can exist. In every moment you are giving energy out and at the same time receiving energy. Your emotions show you whether you're living in the energy of fear or love. For example, the energy of anxiety controls you and is essentially fear in another form. Fear and love are the foundation of all emotions and they are both very powerful. The energy of fear is imprisoning and suffocating; it feels physically restrictive. It is the opposite of being free. Love, on the other hand, is light and freeing. The physical feeling of love is expansive. As your awareness grows you see the truth in these words and in these two energies, for as your awareness expands so do your thoughts, actions and choices. Remember, love is expansive, so to allow more love into your life you must expand to allow it in. The more you expand the more light and love you can allow in. This gives a better idea of why you hear the expression "expanding your awareness." The opposite of this can be described as being closed-minded. Being closed-minded means to allow only a limited number of ideas, beliefs and experiences into your awareness. Where you limit your life in these areas you also don't allow yourself to grow to your highest potential. At this highest level you are living your "ultimate life," or, as we have called it, living your "heaven on earth."

The potential for all beings has no limit. Once you reach one level you will continue up. There is no glass ceiling from a soul perspective or human experience. As you grow you then attract people and experiences that are in line with your level of energy. As you unearth the real you the old experience of you melts away to create the new experience. Life transforms to unearth a world that mirrors the new you. We say the "new" you but essentially it is the "real" you. As your awareness grows you unearth more of who you really are, which is the true you at a soul level. This is part of the purpose of this physical world and why we continue to come back in different lifetimes. To unearth who we really are. Each life chips away at the stone to reveal the beautiful piece of art that you are. You may feel fear with this big change but it is only through change, through this transformation that your ultimate reality can reveal itself. Embrace this change and let go of your fear.

Why is it that we ask for things from the universe and then when we receive them we are afraid? It is because change is the unknown in our mind. It can be our ultimate dream but the newness of it can bring fear, as we have not experienced this before. Fear can quickly turn to excitement and a sense of security.

You hold the power. Take a breath and relax. You are safe and protected. Your security is your faith in life. This realization can cause distress to your mental state or alternatively bring you a great sense of power. Not power in the sense of being better than anyone or anything, not power in the sense of control, but power in the sense of freedom and security. Power with, not power over. A power knowing that you hold the key to everything around you. You hold the power to your thoughts, emotions, feelings, existence and your reality. Everything can change in an instant. You can live your ultimate fantasy or your ultimate nightmare. Nothing can change, nothing can be unless you make it so. Let go of your fear and attachments. That is when transformation happens. You are the only person holding back the universe from transforming your experience into your ultimate heaven on earth. This is not about wanting, searching or needing. This is about being and understanding the truth in the false. This is being aware. Where you find truth you find peace and happiness. This is where your mind is free of the chains of fear. Peace and freedom lie beyond your fear. When you are aware you are free. You are free from the hold of the false. Free of the disillusion of the mind. Free of the ties that bind you to people, to situations and to things that are not conducive to achieving your higher purpose. You then flow with the winds of change easily and peacefully. You embrace anything and everything life brings to you, whether you view this as good or bad.

The truth is nothing life brings you is "bad." Everything occurs to expand your awareness, bring you back to who you really are and help you create your heaven on earth. This is the truth to all experiences and people that come into your life. People show up perfectly at the right time and place to assist you in your higher growth. As their purpose is fulfilled, people and things may go, but revel in the fact that this is for your greatest good. Trying to hold on to things that have no further purpose can only bring suffering into your life. Make room for someone or something greater, which will, in turn, bring you an even greater experience.

Decision Making

What drives your decision? Looking for an answer? When will you find it? Do decisions come easily to you or are you indecisive?

Every moment gives you the opportunity to make decisions, to make choices; choices about what to do, what to think, what to give, how to feel, who you want to spend your time with, what you want to do next.

There is a process going on inside of you every second that you are breathing and living. Something inside of you drives you to be who you are, to feel what you feel, to think what you think about, to act and to be. Your thoughts, feelings and emotions are driven by your stored experience, which is your memory of the past. Your past experiences are your driving motivation for your decision making today. Thus the past is directly in correlation with your now and your now is in direct correlation to your future. Can you understand this? Your past experiences are affecting you right now. They are affecting your views on life. They are affecting your choices and how you react to people and situations. Your past is affecting your emotions and feelings today. For most of you, your past affects your happiness and peace in the current moment. What you are feeling and experiencing now is then correlated to what you will experience, choose and feel in the future.

Humans tend to carry the past, as well as the now, forward. So for most, life can be a circular process, meaning you are just going in circles, experiencing the same experiences and the same feelings without change. When you walk in circles you are for the most part staying the same and staying in the same position. Even though you are moving, you are not advancing or getting to a new location. This can be related to your financial situation, your relationships, your experiences and also your level of happiness or peace. Where you are not changing you are staying the same. Where you are staying the same you are not experiencing anything different. You are not advancing. You may be content and happy with your current state of affairs but the natural state of life is to advance or expand. Not in the sense of success or what you have in terms of physical things but in the advancement of the natural state of energy. The universal energy that governs life, that creates, that destroys is naturally always flowing forward or always moving to advance life in every

aspect. So to flow with this natural state of energy is to be in balance. When you are in balance you are in the ultimate state of happiness, joy and peace. To fight against this natural flow of advancement is to be out of sync with the natural energy. This creates imbalance, which equates to internal conflict or unhappiness, lack of fulfillment or anxiety.

Humans tend to grasp onto what is stable or not moving. This brings a sense of security to the psyche, which is your mind. Again, the natural state is always moving, changing or advancing for the better. So to hold onto the unchanging is unnatural and brings with it conflict and suffering.

Let's further digest the thought that everything is moving or changing. In this physical 3D world, which is life, nothing is eternal, which means nothing is meant to stay the same or stay forever. People, places, objects and experiences are constantly changing due to the natural state of the universe. To try to hold on to one person, place, thing or experience for security will ultimately at some point bring you hardship when that person, place, thing or experience changes, or dies, or leaves, or is lost or is no longer available to you. If your security or happiness is based on something physical when you lose it your sense of security and happiness is then lost which causes unhappiness and suffering in your psyche.

This is all explained to help you understand that the way we are created is amazing. We are given happiness, peace, love, completeness, perfection, joy and abundance right off the bat. It is included with the package. It is like when you buy a new toy and you find that the batteries are not included. You have to go out again and find/buy batteries in order to complete and therefore enjoy this new toy. You were given all that is source when you were created. So to think that life is meant to find, acquire or achieve these things through your experience is false. If you have love now you will create more in the future. When speaking of love we don't mean the love of another or in a relationship. We speak of the feeling of love. The great thing about it is you can change this at any moment. If you didn't have love a minute ago you can have it now. To feel love is to have it. Love is not based on whether you are in a relationship or not. Many who are in a relationship still do not have love. Love is a feeling. If you want to feel more love then the answer is to give more love. When you give the love you want to feel, you then find that you have always had it within. You have never lacked love. You just have forgotten or not realized it was within your grasp. When you are giving it and feeling it your experience then changes. That is when the universal energy has to conform to what you internally are feeling. Then your experience creates more of this. Your internal feelings give the universe direction on what to create in your future. So give love in the moment and you change everything. When you are giving love, and thus feeling it, you bring people into your life that will mirror this love. The people and relationships you experience are only a mirror of what you are giving and feeling. This holds true not only for love but also for everything in life. This is true for your financial state, your success, your happiness, your joy and what you have. You don't need more money or things to feel complete, be happier or experience great things. When you feel abundant and give abundance to others you create more abundance for yourself. The universe will then bring you more money, or things, or happy experiences. That is why you should never have worry or fear about money, physical things or people. When you feel like you have enough money, you give more and don't worry about experiencing things due to the lack of money. In this state of feeling you then bring in more money to continue this abundance you feel. Give in every aspect like you have an abundance of it to give. When you feel abundant you will be more abundant in the next moment.

Back to decision making... When you have the past affecting your mind, emotions, feelings, actions and thoughts your decisions are then based on what happened in the past. Your decisions are then skewed. You fear that things in the past will happen again. You also base your decisions on trying to prevent things from happening again. Because you fear an outcome you make decisions based on trying to prevent the past from happening again. To make the best decision you must have a mind that is clear. Clear from the past and clear from all fear. The best decision will bring you your ultimate happiness, peace, love and joy. If you are feeling hardship or suffering due to your decisions, you're not making the best decisions. When you are consumed by fear it will distort your thoughts and cause you to make decisions that are not the best for your highest good. In this case, usually, any decision you make will bring some sort of suffering since you are afraid of making any decision.

Birth and Death

The soul bound to light is always lit by the source of everything, the source of being, the universal oneness. You can see this as everything that inhabits the universe, heaven and God. You are comprised of energy. A never-ending radiation of pure light energy. This is who you are. You came from the ultimate light source, and when you connect back to this light source, you revitalize or come to your place of peace and joy. This is the ultimate purest love.

Most humans cannot even fathom what this purest form of love is. As a human, parent, partner you are driven by one thing and that is love. This love is tainted by your attachments, your fears, your experiences and your desires. You see they all start with "your." These only have to do with yourself and the conflict within yourself. In reality, you tend to think your attachments, fears, desires and sufferings are the fault of everyone but yourself. Your circumstances, families, friends, relationships cause you to experience the "bad." The truth is that your circumstances and relationships are all bringing out the aspects of who you are being and who you must experience to return back to your light source.

Remember, everything is just a mirror of yourself. Your experience is just a direct representation of who you are being and what you are thinking. You have just as much control of your experience on earth as you do in heaven. The only difference is on earth the manifestation of the physical takes longer. Meaning the timing between your thoughts turning into your reality has a slower correlation time. Your thoughts and imagination are your tools in life. You can only create physically what you are thinking and giving. For example, if you have a car accident, you powered this event to occur. You in a sense manifested it due to your thoughts and actions. Events like a car accident cannot occur without the energy behind it. In heaven thought is instant. If you think of something it immediately creates itself. You learn quickly how to control your thoughts. It is more difficult to learn this on earth. Most of you have no idea that you are creating what occurs in your life. What energy causes hardship, conflict, suffering and separation in your reality? The answer is fear. Fear then creates anger, impatience, selfishness and greed. Fear is the main culprit since fear is the reason behind all these negative emotions.

To hoard possessions or money or to take more than you need is greed. You do not feel there is enough and you need all these things or money for yourself to survive. Yes, to survive. It is a deception of your mind to think you "need" a certain amount of things or money to maintain your happiness, peace and joy. Technically, unconsciously your "life" depends on it. A lifestyle is not based on survival but your mind tends to associate the two. Balance is not based on anything physical. To have balance within oneself you do not "need" anything. It is the point at which you can become aware of this that balance is forming. When your mind, body and soul are in balance is when you do not "need" anything. At this point, the need to give is your driving force, not the need to acquire or attain anything. It is in the state of balance where your ultimate knowing occurs. You approach and react to situations in a way that creates the best possible outcome. Your decisions are divinely guided and you make the decisions to create peace and happiness for you and the people around you.

Death as in birth is interchangeable. It is but a transition from one dimension to another. When you are born you must leave the "ultimate" reality—known as "heaven" by humans—to come into the "physical" reality, which is life as we know it. You could see it as an emersion of your light self into your physical self on earth. Then when you leave the physical body you are re-entering the dimension of light. We are eternal beings. There is never a point where your soul dies or is non-existent. Death is again but a transition. Your higher self or soul is moving from one dimension to another dimension. Your physical body is the only thing that dies and becomes non-existent. What has death meant to you up until this point in your life? How do you perceive death? When we can find an awareness of something or see it for what it really is we find understanding. To understand something we then emerge from the unknown into the known. What we know we do not fear. It is only the unknown where our fear arises. This is true with death. As a human, we see death as something we don't fully understand or know. All we know is it is an end of something that was physical. What we had is no longer there. Life ends and with it, that being we are connected to is gone, in our minds forever.

You cannot fully define who you are as the person you are in this life. Your name, body, physical character, personality, likes and dislikes are only who you are now in this lifetime. The real you or your higher self is much more than what we are aware of. When you move from this life to the next dimension you once again regain the awareness of your higher self. It is merely remembering your higher self or who you really are.

The mind is not immediately conscious of your higher self. It was meant to work that way. If you were able to have the full awareness you do in heaven there would be no point to the transition into the physical world. The goal of your soul is to regain the awareness of your higher self through your life experience. Your life, the experiences you've had, the people that have been a part of it, your personality, your physicality are all created by you so that it may assist you in regaining the awareness of yourself at the heavenly level. You are becoming more whole or complete because of this life. You are becoming all-knowing. By experiencing all you then gain knowledge of all.

You see "God" or Source as the ultimate all-knowing power. The ironic thing is you and everyone in existence and that has ever existed, human or animal is the expression of source. You at your purest self, your higher self, have the same power as this "God" figure. The human mind searching to find a connection with the light source that is heaven, created the idea of God, as we know it, to try to define this ultimate light source. To define the energy that is all that is and ever was we used an image that we can relate to. We created the image of God as appearing as a human being. This higher being that created all and controls all. This helps our limited awareness find understanding in something that is unknown. Even in your physical state, even though you are not aware that you have the same powers.

You are the creator and destroyer of your life and have the power to do the same to others. You have the choice to destroy and kill each other, to kill animals, to kill the earth. You are an all-knowing being. You have all the answers to life, to death and to heaven. You have just forgotten. You also have the power to create. You create life with your love. You give birth to new life and also sadly take the life of others every day. You personally may not have but people all over the earth are doing this every second of every moment. In every moment everyone on the planet has the opportunity to make choices. You have the choice to hate others, to hurt others, to be kind to others, to express your passions, to eat, to pray, to love. The choices you make in every moment create consequences beyond what you can fathom.

We cannot change the world unless you—and every single person on the planet—become aware that you hold the key to changing the entire world. You and you alone. Once you let go of your fear and change your thoughts, actions and words you change the energy that you emit and it will radiate out into the universe. Energy never stops. It's eternally radiating. So the energy you give in every moment is sent out and continues to grow and grow and travels farther and farther until it radiates out into the universe and even beyond our universe. It crosses dimensions of time and space. It then comes back. Back through time and space, back into our universe, back to the earth, right back to the very source that released it. You may feel its touch again in five minutes, five days, five years or maybe not for five lifetimes, but it will return to you and manifest itself as the energy that you released it as. If you release judgment it will return to you as judgment against yourself. If you release understanding, it will return back to another giving you understanding. If you release fear, you will receive more things that give you fear.

You are all walking around on earth in a state of amnesia. Blindly trying to find your way back to the light, which is the state of ultimate happiness, peace, love and joy. Your guiding force in life is this natural guide. You are all vying to gain or find happiness and love. This driving force inside of you is thus motivated by all your actions, experiences, decisions and beliefs. The motivation is the same for everybody on earth. It is the experiences, the people and the environment that distorts this driving force. So you then go about finding this light in different ways. Some of you are so deceived that you think you must find this in ways that only bring you suffering and hardship. So in trying to find this state of happiness, peace and love you inadvertently find more pain, hurt and suffering.

The universal energies govern the laws in this physical plane or as you know it earth. There are natural laws that are there to assist you in your goal of finding your true self and thus living this ultimate state of happiness. If they are not followed correctly they will create the opposite of happiness and peace. These energies destroy you, your families, your societies, your countries, your earth and the entire world. You use the term "evil" to describe this energy. As Book 1 states, evil as you know it does not exist. No one is evil. I guess you could define evil as something going against the natural universal law. Energy is the governing force on earth. It has a natural flow. It flows in a positive direction always redirecting life to the state of balance and harmony. It is in effect to help guide life back to its natural state of pure light, which is the state of heaven. When you oppose this natural energy you create an unnatural pull. It's like trying to push two magnets together on opposing sides. They naturally fight against each other and will not connect. This can be viewed as confliction. There is a conflict of interest you could say between the natural interest of the universe and the interest of the opposing party. There is no way to change this natural law of energy. It is impossible. The more you try the more conflict you create for yourself. When you can let go and conform to the natural flow, the natural energy will take you along with it swiftly and easily to the source of light, thus to a state of harmony, balance and the ultimate state of being. This is the goal of the soul. This is your instinct pulling you to your higher purpose. There is security in knowing negative energy or opposing parties will not last. The natural law of the universe is to dissolve fear and suffering and bring everything back to love and light. Love and light will always find its way back. Even if it appears as if love and light are being overtaken, trust in the fact that the universal law will not allow it.

The Mirror of Life

Anxiety is fear, nothing more. The root of anxiety is fear. Fear kills everything in its path. The source of all the problems in your life and in the world is all based on fear. You fear what has happened. You fear the future. You fear your actions. You fear what is in the moment. You fear making decisions. You fear people, places and things. You fear you're not maintaining the image of yourself. So what do you do? You fester in a pool of your fearful thoughts, which creates anxiety and dysfunction in your life. As a whole, you are not happy. You are not content. You feel alone, empty. What if you could take that fear out of your mind? Fear of everything and anything. What would you do? What decisions would you make? How would you live? And most of all, how would you feel?

When you fear, most of your actions and words are based upon this fear. Anxiety locks you in a cell. It takes away your freedom. This is not who you really are. Who you really are is pure love, perfection, light and happiness. When you are expressing who you really are you are being this pure love, perfection, light and happiness always. When you are being who you really are you radiate this energy always, no matter whom you're around or what situation or circumstances you find yourself in.

People are not being who they really are and then they want others to be this? Is this not an oxymoron? Isn't it easier to be nice or to love someone who is nice and loving to you? Yet you judge, complain, expect, put down and think badly of the people around you. You are anxious, depressed, stressed out, fearful yet you expect your spouse, your children, your families, and the people around you to not be this way. You expect them to be the love, the fearlessness, the support, the comfort and stability. Everything in life is but a mirror. What you are, how you are feeling will directly be represented in your reality, which is your life. We search out people, gurus, therapists and books to help us change and fix our life. The first step to freedom is to look in the mirror. If you want to fix your relationships, marriage, children and life, look in the mirror. It all starts with you not them. When you are free of anxiety, fear, hurt, attachments and greed then you free everyone around you of these things. When you free your mind and soul you free others.

Life is all about your relationships. Not just with people but your relationship with the world around you, with things, with yourself, with thoughts and emotions. Your relationships, your children, your families, your experiences are all mirrors of who you are. Who you are will be directly represented in the people and experiences you have. You cannot expect that your children or your spouse will be something that you are not. If you are angry, fearful, or anxious so shall everybody and everything in your life.

Your life will only mirror back the image of yourself. The hardest thing for you is looking in the mirror. Seeing all the faults, the hurt, the issues, the attachments and the fear. When you look in the mirror you must come face to face with every aspect of the whole or lack thereof which is you. Ironically, the only way to let go and create a fulfilling future is to embrace everything that you hide from. Yes, embrace. Pull out the issues and hurt that you have been burying deep inside yourself and feel it, stare at it and above all love it. This is who you are. This makes you a human and makes you the perfection that you are. The good, the bad, the beautiful and the ugly are all a part of you. It is the sum of everything, which equals you. The more you try to separate the bad, the ugly and the hurt that is a part of you the more you feel incomplete. It's like taking an apple and cutting half of it off because you don't like the color of that half. Well, what then do you have? You have half an apple. If you try to give someone half an apple as a gift they look at you funny. Why would you give me half an apple? Well, why would you give half of yourself to someone? To understand that the imperfections make us perfect is to be all-knowing. When we can embrace the imperfections in ourselves we then can embrace the imperfections in others. This is coming to a place where you find true understanding, patience and humility. You cannot truly give understanding to others when you find imperfection within yourself. Where you are hard on yourself life will mirror that and others will also be hard on you. What you see, you there will find. What you don't see you will not be shown. When you can embrace all of you, so will others.

One of the most common frustrations in life is when life doesn't give us what we want or think we should have. Life isn't being how it "should" be. But life is always showing us who we are being in the moment. So our situation, experiences and relationships are there to help us become aware of who we are and what we are "giving." If you are expressing anxiety and worry, life can only mirror this back. So life will give you more anxiety and worry. You will attract a relationship that is your mirror. As we see, it is all about awareness. Life will constantly awaken you to be more aware of the truth. Our human mind has been so unaware of this process happening but it is the basis of our existence. Awareness is the first step in life. Only when you become aware can you then change your outer experience. For example, you attract a relationship that will mirror who you are and what you are being. This is to assist you in becoming aware of this state of being. It is then when you become aware of this that you can decide if this state of being suits you or doesn't suit you. If it doesn't suit you it is your indicator to change who you are and your state of being. To change your state of being you must change your thoughts, actions and words. This is then how you attract something different into your experience. Again, your outer experience will only mirror your state of being. So change your state of being to be in line with what you want your outer experience to mirror. That is why everything is for your ultimate good. Whether it is "good" or "bad" in your eyes, everything is always working to better your soul and your experience. To guide you to your ultimate state of being, which is your place of balance, peace and happiness.

Where the World Stops and Begins

The place where nothing else exists but the scene around you. Where your senses are heightened by the smells, sounds, feelings and views is where life begins. Where thoughts cease, agendas do not exist and time stops. Have more of these moments. We urge you to experience more of these. This is the world. This is life. This is how we are supposed to live. Where there is passion, love and giving of this energy—this is where truth lies. Truth is just another term for love. When you find truth, you find love. If you have not found love, happiness, peace and joy you have not found the "truth." Many religions claim to be the truth but what do they give? What do they give to the masses? Or better yet, what do they want from the masses? Where there is taking or asking for things from the people such as money and devotion there is no truth. Truth does not ask for anything, truth just is. The truth just gives to give. The truth does not give with the intent to receive. Where there is fear or judgment there is no truth, therefore no love.

That which gives everything but love is false. It is the false parading itself as the truth. What is the answer to every single one of your questions? LOVE. How do you change your life, thus changing the world? Give love. To give as if you have it all is the ultimate truth. In that lies your ultimate happiness. In that lies pure peace. In that lies the highest success.

Do not condemn the already condemned. Meaning, do not judge, hate, despise, threaten, or curse the people, religions and governments that have already condemned themselves. Remember to give love without restrictions for that is the ultimate truth. Love the very people and things that are the opposite of love for they need the most love. Your judgments make you no better and your hate and frustrations only blacken your own experience. It is not their fault. It is just the world's deceptive minds. Where their minds are deceived they spread more deception to the world. Deception breeds suffering and pain. Do not add fuel to the fire that is engulfing the earth. Soothe the hearts that are burning.

The world as it is now will be short lived. The world as you know it will stop and thus begins your heaven. It will not be the world you live in but the heaven that lives in you. The world will just be an expression of your choosing.

Those who do not connect to the love source will make that choice and that will be their experience. Those who do not see the false in the truth will live an experience that is false. Meaning, not their heaven on earth.

You see, it is all a choice. It is as simple as that. Do you choose to see the light in the dark? Do you choose to give love not fear? Do you give others their heaven or do you give them suffering? Where you give others suffering you therefore give yourself suffering. The suffering you give to others will then create an experience of that same suffering for you. Where you steal from another, another will steal from you. Where you lie to someone, someone will then lie to you. Where you rape someone, someone will thus do the same unto you. This can come about in this life or you may experience this in your next life. Thus everything has a reason. Everything experienced has reasoning behind it but what you may not understand is that it is for a good reason.

You experience suffering due to the suffering you caused to your fellow man at some point in time. This suffering is experienced to teach you who you really are. When you cause suffering the only way to truly understand this suffering is for you to experience it yourself. In that, you realize who you really are. This realization is that you are not the suffering. From your own suffering comes humility and compassion. If you are not humble you must experience something that teaches you what humility is because this is who your soul really is. That is why you must be what you want to receive. What you are giving is thus given to you so you can experience who you are being. If you are giving love, you will thus be given that back so you can see who you really are, which is love. Ultimate happiness and peace can only be found through giving because that is the only way you can thus experience states of happiness and peace. Can your mind now see why searching only brings more searching? Happiness, peace and love are not hiding behind a rock. Your happiness does not lie in another's hands. These things can only be found in yourself. To give by using your imagination is to create your next experience.

Earlier, we discussed in the chapter The Mirror of Life, how your life and the people in it are a mirror of yourself. They are all there to show you who you are being and what you are giving. If this is all true you can look at any moment and become aware of what life is telling you. Take a moment to ponder. What have you been experiencing? What have others given to you in terms of your experience and feelings? Have you had physical ailments or sickness?

What is your job and what does this job entail? Through this job, what do you give to employees or to your fellow man?

This can be broken down to the minute details. If you are a manager of a big company, look around you. How is the company set up? How are employees treated? Is the company's goal to give good and happiness or is the goal all financial based? Do you pay your employees minimally to get a higher return? Are you cutting health care to save money? Are your executives being paid millions while other employees struggle? Every employee is a part of the whole, and without them, the outcome would be different. If the executive had to do every position in the company alone it wouldn't work. Therefore, you need everyone in that whole to make it whole, to make it a success.

You too are part of a greater whole. You can dissect your individual life, but when you look at the trickle effect of how many people you alone are affecting the magnitude is greater than you could ever fathom.

This is true from the successful executive to the homeless man on the street. What they both give has the same importance for the whole. It may seem as if the huge executive has a greater effect and importance, but from a divine perspective, everyone has the same importance. No matter who you are, what you do and where you are in life you play an important role for the whole. Every single person affects every other person in the world. Your actions right now in this moment will affect millions upon billions of people. This all happens in a matter of seconds to hours.

Take light as an example. The speed at which light travels is faster than we can even see. It is so fast we cannot see it moving. It is the same for energy. Everything is made of matter; therefore, everything is giving off energy. There is no moment when energy is not moving. Your own energy leaves your body and spreads like big spheres. As it leaves your body it gets bigger and bigger till it is as big as the earth and then spreads out into the atmosphere. So not only are you affecting someone around you physically and mentally, you are giving energy that spreads and ends up touching billions of people, animals and the earth. The energy of the earth is even felt out in the atmosphere. How can you alone change the world? By thinking a thought you are affecting the world. By one action alone you are affecting the entire world.

This little light of mine, I'm going to let it shine, so that all the world may bathe in it. It shall light the dark and remind others of who they really are. What a beautiful thing this little light of mine is.

Shifts in the world are due to shifts in people's thoughts. Let us look at history even just in the last decade. The world has seen many shifts or changes in our cultural and social aspects. How people think and act is constantly changing. The people's views change, thus changing every aspect of life.

Right now man is in a thought revolution. Radical changes in how people think, how people view things, what people believe, what people accept and do not accept are occurring. This is creating a shift in energy. Humans are realizing things are not working for them. It has been millions of years since man has truly been who he really is. We are now coming back to the source of everything. People are uncovering who they really are which man has fervently searched for. Part of this is due to the higher dimensions, which you call "heaven" intervening. Not in a forced sense. Heaven cannot force anything to happen.

That would go against man's free will, which is not love. Control is not love. Ingrain that into your mind. Control is fear-based and thus is as "evil" as any other energy. This intervention is by man's will alone. Humans have been calling for help for ages. This calling has increased rapidly. As man knows, so shall you ask so shall you receive. If you want the answer you will be given an answer. It doesn't matter how impossible it may seem. Everything is possible. There is an answer for everything and a reason for everything. This is a promise given to you. You are never alone and have all the power of heaven with you always, no matter what. When you want an answer it will be given. When you need guidance you will be directed. When you need help, help is there. When you feel alone, an army of love is surrounding you.

There are souls that are sent down to assist man physically. They are placed in physical bodies with a purpose to bring you answers and direction. It is in doing this that they are uncovering more of who they really are and are being able to give love and experience this thing we call life or the physical. It is not that they are higher or better than anyone else. You are all beings of light. Everyone is godly and deserves to be looked at as such because you are all God reincarnated. It is only through

35

you that God is one and therefore can see itself for who it really is which is one and all-knowing. Every human being on the earth is here to assist each other in finding who they really are and to give love to the earth. You are all here to help each other live your heavens on earth.

It is by the choice of your soul that you are here at this time. You chose your physical body, the people around you, the experiences you have had and will have. This was your ultimate vision of perfection to assist you in your purpose and to help you uncover more of who you really are which is pure love and perfection. Perfection in the sense of a whole. Not in the sense of an idealistic definition of perfection. Where you are whole you are one, in balance with the natural state of all, which you may refer to as heaven or the universal oneness. To view yourself as separate pieces is to not be whole. When you dissect yourself by your faults and you separate yourself into pieces, you therefore are not complete.

To be whole also means to have both masculine and feminine energy. The higher energy of the universal oneness is not a male or female. This energy is both feminine and masculine. It is the duality fused as one. When you combine the two it creates a whole. It is by separating the two that you have an imbalance. To see the two as separate entities creates conflict in the mind because it is unnatural. Every person whether they are male or female contains both masculine and feminine energy. You could not be created if you did not.

It is through the fusion of the male and female love that life is possible. It is that creative, non-physical force that is then manifested into something physical. In such, a physical body is created. A soul is then transferred into this physical form. It is the only way that a soul from the higher dimension can experience the physical dimension.

To experience that which you are not, you attract to you another who has the qualities that you lack. For some, this means finding a mate of the same sex. When a male physically has more feminine energy he may search for another male to balance this out. Thus you have a male/male union or a female/female union. This type of union is no different than a female/male union. It is what the soul wants to experience to uncover more of who they really are. This is another example showing you that everything has a reason. It is the choice of the soul on a higher level and in this, they can see in the mirror of life the perfection that they are. It is just God expressing itself in the mirror of life to see itself in all its glory as the perfection it is. Every other human should see through the shroud of deception and be aware of this perfection that everyone is. To see anyone other than perfect is a sin against yourself.

See how the phrase *sin against yourself* is used. You cannot sin against another. The only sin that is made is against yourself. The word sin is not used in terms of doing something bad. It is used in the sense that what you do is doing unto thyself. When you see another imperfectly, the truth is that you view yourself either consciously or unconsciously as imperfect. There is no "bad" being done in life. Your term of "sinful" is false. Everything happening is to help you and others see who they really are. It is only through the "bad" that you can realize who you are being and thus come back to who you really are which is love and light. All the "bad" in the world is a mirror to show each and every one of you who you are being.

What are you thinking and giving? Take a look at the entire world, not just your life. See the devastation, the people and animals suffering and experiencing hardship. This is a mirror of yourself. This is what you are causing due to your thoughts, actions and words. This is the extent of what you are causing. You might laugh at this and call it a bluff, but in only changing yourself, your thoughts, actions and words can you affect others differently, more positively. You cannot change anything but your own thoughts, actions and words. This then gives off a different energy. Like we discussed earlier, your energy is affecting the entire world and even things outside this world.

Fate

Help me to accept the fate I have created. Is it what is meant to be or is it a fate I've created for myself? Could it have been different or was this always what was meant to be? There are always discrepancies. Where in the equation did I go wrong? I guess it is not that anything has gone wrong. It's just what is. I find that some truly are born with luck due to past life circumstances. They are due this goodness, ease and luck in life. No matter the thought or energy they put off it is not affecting them in this life.

For some of us, it is the opposite. Constant trials and tribulations no matter the thoughts, actions or expressions. For those, is this life expressing this due to past life karma? Some are lucky in love but not lucky in experiences. Others are lucky in experiences but not lucky overall. A brief heavenly experience cannot equal a life of love, success and happiness. Can these brief heavenly experiences create happiness when your ongoing life may be filled with less than satisfactory conditions? I ponder that, as I have been blessed with rare heavenly experiences. They have been but brief, whimsical winds that blow through my life. The question is how can I extend these heavenly experiences to become the entirety of my time? Maybe my fate won't allow. I need to be free. Free as the birds in the sky. Free as the fish in the sea. I wish to choose my every moment, to choose the day's adventure.

As humans, we are not free. We are chained by money, chained by our fear, chained by our past karma. The fear can be tackled, but with money, we have no choice it seems. You can't eat, drink and essentially survive without money in the current structure of the world. Because of this, we work over and over monotonously. Isn't insanity doing the same thing over and over again? Why do we care about numbers and rates, how many emails we can complete? Why do I care about systems, emails, dirty dishes and timetables?

The answer? Because there is always an agenda. There is no motivation without an agenda. So we are here with our own agendas to follow. What is the agenda of our soul? I guess we all have our own separate agendas. Billions of people running around like ants with separate agendas trying to function as a whole. I guess that is our problem.

This individual agenda we seek to attain. Maybe the bigger problem is that we have no idea what our individual agenda is. We are trying to attain the agenda of the masses. Do the masses really know what is true? What is right for me and for the whole? I think that is where we get conflicted. Our internal agenda drives us, but our mind is being told something else. So then our souls sit conflicted, unfulfilled and lacking.

I want to meet with the birds and the flowers in the meadow. There we can discuss freedom, happiness, peace and beauty. That is what I care about. This can give more fulfillment and knowledge than any system, any computer, any manager, any CEO, any amount of money or any book. This is where life starts and ends. It starts with the caressing rays of the sun and ends with the call of the loon on the lake.

Birds, please show me the ways of the truly free. Teach me to soar and flow with the wind. You take advantage of the wind so beautifully. Let the wind always believe it is in control, but you know better, my knowledgeable teacher. For giving yourself to the whims of the wind you in truth have the higher power. Give me your secrets. Oh, how lucky you are. Can I do away with this agenda, this idea of happiness, the very definition of insanity? Will I have my sun, my flowers, my birds and my meadow? The magic eight ball says...... Absolutely.

To Forgive but Not Forget

To forgive is the ultimate act of your true divine self. Why must the human mind have such a hard time forgiving the acts of another? If we were expressing who we really are, no act, words or experience would tarnish the light that we are. The soul is untouchable. It is whole as it is. It is only the ego that sees itself as anything else but whole. It is your ego deceiving you into thinking otherwise.

You were created in the image of perfection, just like every human and creature on this earth. Your shape, personality, decisions, actions, words, physical appearance are all perfection for your soul. It is only when we let another make us feel imperfect that we are wounded. We all want acceptance and love from everyone because those things bring us happiness and peace, which are the energy of love. Anything that is harmful, hurtful, painful and angry is not love. All these things slowly kill love and ultimately chip away at the whole, happy, peaceful person that we are.

When we are attacked by another in such a way that it causes us great distress, we often react by causing the same harm to the person who attacked us or possibly to another. We resist forgiving them because we essentially think to do so means we are accepting what was said or done while allowing the other person to continue harming ourselves or others and think that it is okay.

Why would we give such satisfaction to the perpetrator? To hold on to the hurt ironically gives us gratification. Unconsciously, to be the victim fills our ego. So we like to maintain the victim role. If we forgive we are stating we are no longer the victim. It is easy to always point the finger at everyone but yourself. If we take the role of the victim then we are not to blame. To be the cause makes us feel imperfect or that we did something wrong.

We all are driven by the need to be accepted, loved and to find happiness. Every action of every human is based on this drive. Even vengeful, angry, hurtful actions are driven by this basic human need. This may seem sick to the commoner, but the people who feel the most hurt express their needs in this manner. A mind that has been hurt by another enough times will react to defend the whole of who they are. It is natural instinct. This is how you are affected when you hold on to the hurt that has been caused to you. To not forgive is to hold on to the hurt, resentment and anger triggered by another's words or actions. To truly be able to forgive is to let go of this hurt, resentment or anger that you hold on to. To create balance within the self and within your life, it is vital to be free of these energies. Many do not realize that you cause the most harm to yourself rather than to the other when you cannot forgive.

How can you find it in yourself to forgive something you deem unforgivable? You can find this by seeing the reality or the truth behind this person's actions. Can you see beyond the physical into the depths of who this person really is? A being so perfect, so filled with love and light that they are crying out for love and acceptance. Can you view this as the truth and not that they are just mean and selfish humans? They are not aware of what drives them, but they are hurting enough that the only way they feel they can sustain who they are is by reacting in such a way that ends up hurting everyone around them.

By you forgiving them you are not stating that what they did is okay. It is understandable to still express that what happened was not okay even as you choose to forgive.

Forgiving doesn't mean you are condoning behavior, it means you are releasing the ties that bind you to the hurt and to that person—freeing yourself to create a clearer, happier, more balanced life. As you can truly express your forgiveness of this person as a human you will feel the darkness lift off you and find yourself lighter. You can breathe deep and free once again. It is these moments where you show the light that you are. A light so grand, so blinding and beautiful. Here is where you can look in the mirror of life and find perfection expressed right back at you in your heaven, which is your life.

The Secret of Attraction

It's not that it's the wrong time or the right time. It
depends on when you are going to realize the time is now.
When something shows up or appears it's the perfect time.
Relationships are not luck. They become an experience to
show you who you are being. If you don't like what you see
or are not finding the image of what you believe to be
"right" it is because you are not being what is "right." You
are attracted to mirrors of yourself. You find something in
another that ignites an attraction because you
unconsciously see yourself in them.

Every relationship you come across is there for you to
uncover more of you. Uncover what you have been being
and what you are being now. If you do not like what you
see in this person then look inside yourself. The lack in
another or the frustration you get from another is the
same in yourself. The human mind may not realize it but
we don't like the fault in ourselves just as much as we

don't like the faults in another. We are not here to get love or find love. We are here to give love. If you are not giving love, receiving it back from another will be a challenge. You cannot attract something you are not.

Also remember that you are perfection and have always been. If someone says otherwise it is only due to the imperfections they see in themselves. Imperfections are not real; they are false. Everyone is perfect. It is the deception of the world that has made them see themselves as imperfect, which they then transfer to you. A person who says hurtful words is hurting, and due to their own hurt they unconsciously express the hurt they have in a way that hurts others. You, knowing they are perfect, see the beauty inside the falseness of their actions. Do not take what they say personally, because you know you are perfect. When you know your own perfection, you allow others to see theirs too.

As you change, your relationships will change. You will attract others that are more in line with who you've become. When you first are whole and find balance in yourself, you will then find another who is of like energy. Where you are abundant you attract abundance into your life. Where you worry or fear, you will attract more of that worry or fear. This is especially true in your relationships.

Even if you attract healthy, loving relationships into your life, they will eventually end at their right time. Nothing is meant to last forever in the physical world. Things deteriorate and things die. No one relationship is meant to be "forever." Life is constantly evolving, transforming for the better. People come into your life at certain times to help you see who you are being, whether it is good or bad. To hold on to the bad will only bring suffering and hardship. That is also true for relationships. You may find a relationship to be difficult, full of hard work. The sooner you can be aware of what this mirror is showing you about yourself the sooner you can transform yourself and change the energy in your life, therefore bringing someone else into your life that is more in line with the ultimate truth of a pure love union.

Out of fear you may hold on to relationships that bring your energy force down. Someone of a low energy will only bring your energy down to theirs. If your energy is at a higher level you will naturally only attract people of higher energies. We speak of a "pure love union." A pure love union is that of two people who are of a higher dimensional energy frequency. This is the frequency of ultimate happiness, peace and love. When these two frequencies meet, they experience this state of ultimate happiness, peace and love times two. It is the ultimate union.

People speak of the law of attraction fervently. You reap what you sow. You get what you give. Attraction is an energy. It's like two magnets. You are magnetizing certain energy. That is the answer to all your questions and problems. You cannot attract an energy that is not in line with your own. It is against the natural law of the universe. You are expressing yourself right now. You are giving the world that which you are, your knowledge and your energy. It may not always seem like it, but it is certainly happening in every moment whether you are aware of it or not.

Why haven't you experienced yet what you wish to experience?

There is a reason for all. What you have not experienced doesn't mean you won't. What you have experienced doesn't define you in this moment. It does not have to limit you or make you better than anyone else. You allow your experience to limit you because you let it affect your thoughts, emotions, feelings and actions. When you allow this to happen your experience controls you. You do not have control of the experience. It is only when you have control that you can decide and change what you are experiencing. It may come easier to others, but again, there is a reason for that. Your energy from the past helps create your experience today. Everyone puts in their due time. Don't question that. Where one life seems easier another's is full of hardships.

Live in the light. Hold on to the warmth. Looking into yourself may not always feel natural. It may be uncomfortable. Looking into your own eyes you see all that is you. You see the things you run and hide from, the fears, the hurt, the ugly, the bad and most of all the love. You run from the love inside yourself because you find it best to run from that which you truly want but don't think you can have. That is where you are most vulnerable. That is where you are naked and free. That is the place of pure love. When you allow that place to open up or let someone in you are afraid of them hurting or rejecting that pure part of yourself. The moment you allow that essence of yourself to be penetrated it is almost too good to be true. We are conditioned to believe something too good to be true is always a delusion. That life is lived by conditions, social norms and the expectations of others. Life should be anything but that. Where we live by the expectations of society and our families we limit ourselves to a life that is just so-so. In these conditions, we are not expressing who we truly are (which is pure love). When we are free to be who we truly are and make decisions based on our soul's prerogative, we find true happiness, peace and joy. There are no rules to life. The only advice that can be given is to give love. It's as simple as that.

The Elemental Table

Life is such that what you are experiencing is what you are giving to the world around you. If you experience anxiety that is what you have been giving to the people you come in contact with and the world around you. What you experience is what you've caused; therefore, you must receive it back. Can you understand this concept? What you give is what you get back. This is vital to your transformation. To transform things, to experience something new you first must give it. That is the key to the experience of life. There really are instructions to life.

Energy is the creative force in the physical world. If there were no energy the physical world would be stagnant. You give instructions on your experience by the energy you give. To feel angst is to create more angst. To be depressed is to create more depression. To live in fear is to create more fearful experiences. To feel the lack of something is to create more of the experience of not having. Do you see?

How do you change things? How do you create something new? You give the energy you want out to the universe.

For example, if you lack in the financial department you tend to focus on that lack by not giving to others financially, by hoarding your money, by not living abundantly. You worry about money and fear you won't ever have enough. This is the energy you are feeding to the universe. The universe does not know how to differentiate negative from positive or what you want and don't want. Your energy is your wish given to the universe, your personal genie.

In addition to knowing what energy you are putting out, you must be clear about your ultimate intention. Are your intentions purely for yourself? Are your intentions only for yourself and your spouse and family? If so, you are limiting the energy you give. To give based on restrictions is limiting the abundance you bring forth into your life. Those who give to the entirety of their fellow man, family or foe will experience the true abundance of the universe. To expand it further, if you limit your love to just one person you are not giving to your fullest potential. Essentially, you are putting limits to your love. Then in return, the universe will give back to you on a limited basis.

The abundance of the universe is limitless. Do you want limitless abundance or limited abundance? To give to your fellow man, animals and nature is harnessing the ultimate truth. In this state of giving you are finding the ultimate power of happiness and abundance. To be abundant in all aspects of divinity is a place that most don't bother to trek due to the limitations you place on yourself and others and the fear you hold. To put limitations on your thoughts, your mind, your dreams, and your experience you limit the abundance that is your God-given right. It is your choice to have and experience what you will. If you choose not to experience the full abundance that the world can give, that is your choice.

Your life purpose is individually based. Your *higher* purpose is the same as everyone else's. You are all in the physical world for each other. To help everyone else on earth find who they really are. That is why people come into your life at certain times. There is a reason for everyone you have crossed paths with. They were brought to you to show you who you really are and who you are being. They come into your life to hold up a mirror to yourself to help you uncover your true self by helping you find who you really are and who you aren't. That is why when you hang on to another out of fear you create more of what you do not truly want to experience or be. You may act this way due to fear of being alone, fear of consequences, fear of change, or simply feeling obligated because it feels like the loving thing to do. But do not mix up love and emotions. That which is based on emotions is not love. That which is attachment is emotion. Love is not hurt, love is not control, love is not obligation, and love is not attachment. True love is to give freedom and the abundance of happiness, peace and joy. Pure love is allowing another to truly experience who they really are, which is pure love and light.

To give laughter to another is to bring more laughter into your life.

To put a smile on another's face is to put a smile on your own.

To give money as you have an endless supply will then give you the reality of having an endless supply of money.

To give someone the ability to be honest without condemning him or her is to bring someone into your life that will give you the same acceptance.

To give another pure love without expecting it back will bring you a love that will give you the same pure love.

To see life as heaven on earth is to create an experience for yourself that is your heaven on earth.

To be positive in the face of hardships will bring you positive experiences instead of negative.

To know is to find fact in something, which is then made true in your experience.

To only focus on the trivial things in life is to limit yourself to the beauty of the whole experience. When you are not taking in the full beauty of life, you are not whole, therefore causing feelings of unfulfillment, keeping true peace and happiness out of your reach.

But even if you struggle with these feelings, you are perfection. At your core soulful self, you are faultless, whole, radiant and beautiful. It is your thoughts, actions and words that make you appear imperfect. How can you be called perfect if your thoughts, actions and words are imperfect you ask? It is because your mind deceives you. The people, environment, situations and experiences you have are filtered through your mind. Your mind makes you believe the false in all of these things which then conditions you to think and react in imperfect ways. I guess you could say we are all imperfectly perfect. If you could see the truth in this statement it would change the way you think, act and speak.

The Lark

Shall we begin with the ending? When we begin with the ending we decide how we want things to end. Then for the beginning and middle of the story, we can add what is needed to create the outcome we are looking for. If you don't know what you want, you'll have a hard time directing life to bring it to you. Life responds to your requests. It creates experiences and brings things forth that you direct it to.

Many people are now aware of the concept of manifestation or creating your reality. This has been a major part of the new age movement. You are hearing it all over the place, in books and in the media. Spiritualists are spreading this concept to the masses. Why you ask? Because it is the fundamental law of energy. It is the why and how to life. Why is this happening to me? How can I get this or change this? The answer to most of life's questions lies in the concept of manifestation. You and you alone create every experience, circumstance and relationship in your life. The sooner you understand this and use it, the sooner you'll have control of the now and the future. You may not be able to change the past, but you certainly created everything in it. It all happened the way it did due to your actions and the energy you expressed.

What happens in your life is a direct correlation to the energy you are expressing. You express energy in your thoughts, actions and words. You can think because of energy. You can walk because of energy. Without energy, there would be no life. You would not be able to move or talk. Life could not express itself in the physical world without it. Your energy is constantly creating what you are experiencing now and what you will experience in the next five minutes, the next hour or the next year. This concept is a very lengthy subject, and, as you can see, we will discuss it many times in many chapters. It is very important to metaphysical understanding and to every aspect of life.

The ending of the story is the best part. It is the end all, be all. The result of all the series of events in the story. It is what we pine and toil for. We go through the steps only to create an outcome. In the fairytales, we want to hear the story because we know that in the end, we will get everything our hearts' desire.

61

If you can dream you can create. All dreams big and small started with a desire or a thought. It is the energy to create something physical. If you can dream it, it is possible. Truly, energy is like magic. It is the unknown that creates something from nothing. It is the impossible becoming possible.

If you feel lost on this journey of creation, let the lark show you the way. There are guides everywhere, showing you the way. You just don't pay any attention to them. Where you find meaning and importance in the tangible things you discredit life. Life is so much more wonderful and abundant than you give it credit for. Again, what you place meaning and energy on controls you. Here is a question: day to day, what do you place your thoughts and energy on? Write these down. Take a look at these things. In the grand scheme of life and all your dreams, how significant are these? Probably less significant than a grain of sand in the ocean. For example, think of how much time you spend reading and responding to emails. If you can think of your grandest dream you could ever imagine, where do emails rate compared to this dream? Probably very low. If you were to die and go to heaven today do you think these emails would have any importance to the advancement of your soul? This truly shows you how we place meaning in things on a day-to-day basis that really mean nothing yet consume our existence.

The only reason we are on this earth living this life is to advance our soul. In this form, living your story you are advancing your soul. You were given the physical body, the people and the circumstances all to help assist you on your soul's journey. This life is the most important thing to your soul, as it is only through this life that your soul can advance to the level needed to become more "God"-like. When we speak of "God" it means the universal energy of everything that is a part of the one. When I say "one" I'm referring to everything in existence on the earth, in the galaxy, in the universe in all dimensions of heaven and light. There is so much more to the "one" than your mind can fathom. To open your awareness is to open your mind's capabilities to take in more knowledge and understanding of everything that is a part of the "All" that is life, that is heaven. Without the openness to anything and everything, the answers you seek can never truly be found and understood. In reality, you want the answers, but you don't want to hear them. But all knowledge and energy should be used to your advantage; to make your life better, to create a better existence for you and everyone around you.

Where there is knowledge there is power. Power in the sense of being able to create the story however you so choose. When the term power is used it is never in the sense of controlling others to gain or take. You are most powerful where you are independent, fulfilled, happy, loving and at peace. In this state of power, no other person or experience has any sway against your state of being. Where you can maintain balance at all times, in all situations, among all people. That is truly powerful.

When in your power, nothing is seen as bad or viewed as a hardship. You know that all people are perfection in your eyes and are there in whatever form they take to help your soul be better. Out of their love for you, they show up to help you see the same light within yourself. This is a soul contract that you created with each other. It is through your perspective of them that they then can connect to that same light within themselves. Or, on the opposite end, they could be more deceived about who they really are. No one is bad or evil. People express or show themselves as they see the world or as others have treated them. Other people and experiences have deceived them. That is why we are all so different in our ideas, beliefs, attitudes, actions and most of all how we react to life.

How you choose to react to life is up to you. How you choose to live in your power (or not) is your decision. Finding peace, living the life you want, creating the ending you desire—it's all up to you to choose it. Like the lark, you are free to journey to whichever destination you desire. You are free to slow down and really see all the beauty that is around you in this moment.

The lark exemplifies the freedom, beauty and essence of the theme of this chapter. The most insignificant of things bring forth the most meaning. The lark sitting on the branch can bring more meaning than the fast-paced lifestyles you live. Take time out to immerse yourself in the nature all around you. You want to connect with the higher energies? You want to find the peace you are looking for? Watch the lark, watch the ripples of the lake, and watch the wind blow through the trees. This will connect you with the knowledge you need to learn.

The Ego

The ego is our own worst enemy. The ego deceives our mind. The mind is a great tool to be used and was given to us to be the captain of our ship. The power within us resides in all our senses. It is the mind that is the creative powerhouse. It is what we need to live out our heaven on earth. The ego is a part of the mind. The ego is constantly interfering with our mind and heart. Any thought that is negative comes from the ego. The essence of the term "evil" was created by the ego. When we compare or judge we are doing this through the ego. To view anything as not perfect is only the ego deceiving us. The ego is a manipulator and most of us actually only function off of our ego. To be aware of the ego is the first step in changing the course of your life. It is the same as being aware of every thought that you think. Where you are in control of your thoughts you are able to use the mind to your advantage to create whatever you want in your life. Where you let your thoughts and ego control your words and actions you live on automatic pilot. Whatever comes to your mind you automatically react with words or actions. This is not being in control of your life. Where you are not in control you experience things that are not fulfilling or that express your true self.

In the dimension of heaven, there is only one sense, whereas on earth most of us have five senses. Some who are more aware have six senses. The soul in the heavenly dimension only knows the energy of pure love. There is no thought in this realm. Thought only comes in the dimension of time and space, which is what we experience in the physical realm.

As we discussed the meaning of "time" in Book 1, time is thought that comes from comparing the past, present and future. Thought is just the measurement of experience. A comparison of what was, what is and what should be. This comparison is the root of our internal conflicts. In human terms, it's the cause of anxieties, depression, emotional dysfunction, physical ailments and disease. In heaven, there is nothing to compare because time is not present in the soul. The soul is just eternally experiencing oneness and love. We see the dimension our soul passes into as "heaven" or this place of peace, love, happiness and joy. As we awaken from our "death" or passing in the next dimension, we realize the physical plane or earth is "heaven" as well. It is a place where we can experience the eternal oneness with six senses instead of one. How heavenly is that? Sounds pretty great, doesn't it? To be able to experience the energy of love physically. To taste love, touch or feel love, see love, hear love. Here we can emotionally connect with something physical. We are birthed with the paintbrush in our hand. Here we are in this oasis of the physical where we are able to experience whatever we wish. You are not alone in this physical experience. There are billions of other souls being reborn with you to share in this wonderful experience. If you could read the book of all your lifetimes, oh, how captivated you would be!

Every human has a choice. The choice to be, to give, to think, to be aware, to feel and to experience whatever your heart desires. You alone make the choices in your life that have created your whole experience. It is just that most of you have created a life with no awareness of what is really happening and the truth to this whole thing called life. So you may label your experience thus far as bad or hard. Everything that has occurred in life or is occurring has been created by the human mind. What humans have created includes natural disasters, weather, global struggles and hardship, disease, physical pain and individual struggles. You have willed it all to be. But you can also will it all to be different.

The first step to overcome the ego is to become aware of this concept. You and you alone have willed the good, the bad and the pain. If you have physical struggles in your life whether it be a backache or sickness, your mind created this experience for you. When you can take ownership of this, you can heal it. This can be difficult for some because they don't want to essentially be punished unconsciously for doing bad deeds.

The ego is part of our unconscious mind. We are not fully aware of the ego when it is working and coming into play in our experience. The ego wants to be strong, perfect and wants to point the finger at everything and everyone but ourselves because that would indicate to the ego that we have done wrong. The ego thrives off living in the victim role. The ego sees itself as a victim—to our experiences, the outside world and to others. Whether it be our disease, our relationships, our lifestyles, our experiences or our pain—it is all out of our control. When someone causes us pain either emotionally or physically it is not our fault, and the ego holds on to this. It is nothing but the deception of the ego that causes us to think and react in the ways we do to outside influences in a negative way. Where we can't

69

forgive, it is because of our ego. It is nothing else, for the soul and heart cannot be hurt. They cannot be diminished or tainted.

You may be reading and not believing these words, but it may be that you are not ready to let go of the things that are holding you back. You may not see instant gratification to the change in your awareness and the changes you have made but it doesn't mean life is not conspiring currently on your behalf. Where you change instantly the energy shift is instant. Awareness is instant. That is why you hear every moment is an opportunity to change everything. Your entire life may not change instantly because heaven, like a painting, unearths itself in every moment. Your physical sense could not handle such a huge shift that fast. That is why it unearths itself in perfect time so that you may marinate in the beauty unfolding in front of your eyes. You may question yourself but inside you know without a doubt that your heaven is right in front of you.

Let's look further into the many faces of the ego and see where it likes to show itself. Become aware when your ego is coming out so you can no longer be controlled by it.

Judgments

Most people may claim they are not judgmental, but in every moment we may not be noticing how much and how often we have judgmental thoughts. We may not always speak or act out our judgments, but here we are pinpointing the ego in action. Judging someone or a situation is stating that this person or situation is not perfect. That in your eyes there is something not up to your standards or that you view as bad or incorrect. Pointing out the bad or inadequacies in another is in a sense judging them. Everyone is perfectly made just the way they are. With both the good and the bad. So when you find yourself complaining or seeing faults in another whether it be your friends, family, co-workers, or strangers on the street, your ego is in action. See beneath the personality, actions, choices and physical appearance of others. Behind this façade is a perfect soul in search of love and acceptance. When you can see this perfection in everything, no matter what you see on the outside, you see the truth. A façade is the outer deception. To function with this awareness is assisting you in creating peace, balance and your heaven on earth. Again, what you see is what you get. So where you see perfection in others they morph to show you that perfection. Where you see lack and imperfection life will create more people and situations on your path that mirror this.

Being Hurt

When we are hurt by another's words or actions it is only the ego that is affected. The ego deceives us into thinking we are lacking or makes us believe the words of another in regards to ourselves is true. If someone points out a fault of ours we feel attacked or victimized, which causes us to see ourselves as not good enough or imperfect. But as this person is judging us it is only their ego in action. Ego is not real. It causes us to think, speak and act in ways that are not real. The ego acts out to protect ourselves and feeds the idea that we are not perfect. Where we see ourselves as imperfect we see others as imperfect. Our actions and words are a mirror of what is happening internally. When we cause hurt to others we are therefore hurting inside and expressing this hurt. We can see through the exterior actions and words of others, as it is just their ego maintaining itself. When we can see this truth we relinquish the hurt and suffering within ourselves. Life as it stands currently is a continuous battle of the egos. We can only stop it when we can become aware of this.

Comparing & Contrasting

The ego is constantly comparing us to others. Comparing what we have and what we are experiencing to what is going on around us. The ego is telling our mind that we are lacking in some aspect. That we are not good enough. Ultimately, that we are not perfect and our life is unfulfilling. Comparisons bring up feelings of resentment, envy, jealousy and greediness. The ego in this sense brainwashes us to think there is not enough to go around. There is not enough money, relationships, jobs, success, food and material items to go around. We see someone have something we don't and we want it for ourselves. Since we don't have what they have in the present we see lack in our life. Again, this is the ego deceiving us. The physical is abundant in every aspect. What someone has you can also have. There is enough food to feed everyone in the world and then some. The physical is a place of manifesting anything and everything. That is what our mind is for. Your mind has the power to create anything out of nothing. You don't need to have it physically right now to know it is possible. See and feel the abundance around you happening in every moment. The more you see life as abundant the more life will mirror that abundance in your life in every aspect. When we are able to see

73

another have something that we may want or desire, it is life proving to us that it is possible. Where one is abundant or prosperous so are we all. This should bring comfort and hope to the mind. It is only when we let the ego rule that we see the false in this truth.

What We Know of Being

How does a human mind define being? Can you truly understand what it is to be? I guess to be is to live, but what we now know of living is not truly being. The human mind sees living as working, attaining, creating and surviving. We can break each of these down into further categories.

Take attaining. We live to attain money, relationships, objects, success or attaining an image of oneself. In your mind, you search to attain, to give you fulfillment, completeness and reassurance of who you are. When your physical experience is telling you or showing you something you then believe it in your mind. You can't believe you are successful until you get reassurance from other people or from the amount in your bank account.

Now let's look at animals. They see living differently than humans. They are not living. They are being. That is the difference between the two. Their sense of being does not lie in anything and is not defined by anything but the essence of breathing and being in the physical experience humans call life. Something physical does not give it truth and something non-physical does not make it false. The physical things around you that you call life are not the truth and the non-physical that you call heaven is not false.

The human mind has taken the essence of being and distorted it and separated it. The mind and heart now find much confusion in the whole experience of this thing called life. The human experience is only what you have created, and aren't all of our experiences different? It is a series of events that you have created. The bad, the good, the distortion and the truth you find in it. To find purpose in something that is false creates conflict and hardship for the mind, body and heart. You find purpose in a monetary system of exchange and label it as the truth and this creates nothing but conflict and hardship for the world and for yourself. Find wherein your conflicts lie and there you will find the false of life. You label truth to something that is false and distorted and of course it will cause you conflict and hardship.

You find purpose in a cycle of actions or "work," as you call it, that does nothing for the soul and creates conflict and hardship. The human idea of "work" to us is just a monotonous cycle of the same action attempting to get the same result or a consistently improving result. Most of you define this work as necessary to attain another falsity, which is more "physical" things, which as we know is a falsity of our experience. Most of the actions of the world are based on the attainment of physical things. If the only intent behind your actions were to be, it would transform the world.

To be is to live where to live is not to be. Our intent is not to just live or to fall victim to the distortion of others' truths. Our intent is to be and find truth within ourselves. Our intent is not to work but to marinate in the experience. Our intent is not to attain but to give the essence of ourselves. Our intent is not to create but to share the love of every person and every thing and relish in the transformative power it holds. Our intent is not to survive but to be a part of something that is beautiful and whole and to sustain our physicality through this beauty.

Look at your life. What things do you feel hold you back from experiencing happiness? Could it be money, love, your job, or your personal relationships? Maybe it's just fear in general. Do you have an abundance of fear pertaining to many aspects of life? Where there is fear or unhappiness there are attachments. You base your happiness on the attachment you have with physical things such as money, objects and people. Then to these things you attach your own expectations. Expectations of what they should be, how much you should have, what they should be giving you. As the truth states, to hold expectations of physical things and people will only give you hardships. So doing this will never bring you happiness and you will never be fulfilled even if you receive what you think you should have.

Take money for example. Where you hold truth to money, you bring yourself conflict. The physical object of money is false. Anything physical is false. There is no truth to money. It is a figment of your imagination. Anything physical is an imagined reality made physical. Everything physical was only made possible because someone created it, not just physically with their hands but through the use of their imagination, which made it a reality. Therefore, everything is only a figment of one human's imagination. The imagination is your tool to create your experience. Anything can be made a reality. Anything. Can you fathom this concept? If it can be imagined it can be created. Think back to 100 years ago. If somebody told you that you could speak and see someone in another country on a screen they would think you were crazy.

Is anyone really crazy? How do you define crazy? Someone who does not think in line with the popular thought maybe? Well, we individually define our view of life and how we think things should be. This also includes people. We define our personal thoughts on how people should think, act and talk. Again, where we label truth we create conflict within our minds and hardship in our experience. There is no truth to anything. Where we find answers we find truth. What we experience or see in the physical we label as truth. What we do not know or have not seen most of us cannot label as truth. This can be good news for the searching mind. Our life is to create our own truth. That is our will. Our will to create an experience to suit our soul's needs. To know something you must experience it. So how can we truly understand death or heaven if we have not experienced it firsthand? The same with heartbreak or depression? How would someone really understand something unless it was experienced? Can this be the same for the soul and our life? How would we truly know what love is unless we experienced it? Could you already be love but just not remember? What if the only way to remember is to experience that which you thought you were not? Let us ponder that a moment.

We place value on everything from a dollar to ourselves to our personal relationships. When we put a higher value on something it holds more of our attention or happiness. Most of us place value on ourselves and therefore work to maintain our existence. When we place less value on ourselves we may succumb to "letting ourselves go." This can be to our physical body or our mental state. Most would put more value on a hundred dollar bill over a one dollar bill. Why is this? Because of the number printed on a piece of paper. Because someone told us this number 100 held more value than the number 1. The higher the number the more you can acquire, correct? The more you have or are able to acquire the better you are? The happier you are? I guess we are just trying to understand all this. You may not think of it this way because all you know and have known is from your conditioning. Try to think from the standpoint of someone who may have never experienced this concept of money or monetary exchange. That through the exchange of paper or coin you receive a physical object or a service from someone. The value placed on this object or experience was created by the masses. The more people that wanted something the greater its value. The higher the value, the greater the attachment held. We hold great attachment to our house because the value is high. The work acquired to attain something like a house is great for most. If we were to lose this it would cause great suffering due to the attachment we have to it and the value we see in it. We hold expectations on this item. We expect it to be there, to maintain its physicality, to bring us good experiences. When it doesn't or is taken away from us we suffer. The level of suffering depends on its value, the expectations we have of it, and how much of a stake it has in our happiness and security.

Don't we have a stake in everything physical in our lives? This can range from our relationships, to our house, to an item of clothing. Why do we value our spouse more than an item of clothing? You may view this as a stupid question. Our spouse holds a stake in our sense of security and provides us with much more than a physical inanimate object. Almost everything provides us with a sense of security. Without these things, our "sense" of security is threatened. We use the word sense because if we lose most things in our life our true security is not threatened. If our spouse leaves us we will not die in a literal sense. If we didn't have a car, again our physical life is not lost. Can you think of all the things in your life and measure the level of "security" you mentally hold to these items or people? What if we didn't attach any sense of security to anything?

What if our security was not attached to our relationships? What if we had no expectations of anyone? Many would respond and say what's the point then? Let's turn this around. How do you feel when people hold expectations of you? Especially high expectations that you find you can never meet? What does this bring to your romantic relationships? This partner expects you to do certain things, to give them certain things, and when you don't it causes conflict. I think everyone has been in that situation where you are being the person they want you to be. Essentially, they are saying I want you to be someone different than who you are because who you are being now is not good enough and does not make me happy.

Being you is enough. Look at yourself in the mirror and tell yourself that you are enough right here, right now. The good and the bad is enough and you release the need to be anything else. Being authentic is all you need to find security. Security is in the trust of yourself and the light that is within you. As you trust in life you don't need others to prove their trust. You are trust. Be that which is you, truly and honestly you. Whatever that is, is beautiful and imperfectly perfect. This is expressing the light that you are when you can be authentically you without judgment, expectations or conditions. It is only here that you can find fulfillment and peace.

There Comes a Day

To describe the indescribable—this is a formidable task. There is nothing that can describe a truth that another is not aware of. How do you make someone aware you ask? You cannot. Awareness comes on its own accord. It is only through the clearing of deceptive energy that one becomes aware. What is this awareness you ask? Why, it is becoming aware of all the answers in the universe. It is becoming aware of the true vibration of life. It is seeing the truth in the false.

Everything going on around you is false. It is a movie. A script created by each and every one of you. There is no reality to it. It is only when you attach reality and truth to the things going on around you that you cause suffering for yourself. Your mind is conflicted in the face of this false play going on around you. Your soul knows all. It knows it is all false. It is only your mind that is sorely conditioned to believe the physical world is real, that what you see is reality. Anything that causes unhappiness, anxiety, stress, negativity, suffering, pain and fear holds no truth. All these negative emotions and feelings have no tangible reality to them. These emotions were created by humans. There is no God or heavenly beings that caused this upon you. You caused this on yourself.

You must open yourself up to any possibility. Anything and everything is possible. You may even have to entertain the thought that all your beliefs, your security, religions and truths may be false. Awareness cannot be defined or labeled as a religion or a belief. Awareness is stepping out of confines and definitions. It is accepting any choice, decision, belief, and action. Maybe, just maybe, everything that you've been searching for has been right in front of you or better stated, within you. That you've been looking for something outside yourself that is really within. That the security you crave is already there. That the morality, the purity, the goodness, the happiness, the peace and above all the love you crave is given to you at birth. You have never lost it. You do not receive it from another. You've had it all along.

The journey thus far is one of insanity, to put it lightly. Our mind longed for the insanity. That is what makes it so sweet. This realization. There comes a day when everything makes sense. Where the indescribable is felt within and such is experienced in the physical. The beauty of the insanity is that it all had to be to bring you to this place of awareness. The insanity awakened you from your temporary amnesia. Security comes from within. Where you are secure on the inside the outer world will conform and physically create experiences that give you security. Pure love comes from within. Where you feel pure love, you thus give pure love. This is where the outer world transforms itself into pure love and you then experience pure love physically from both people and experiences. The list continues.

Trust now in yourself. Never before have you felt the light inside you. This light you feel is your soul. This is who you really are. You hid your own light from yourself. No one else did this to you. You created all the experiences that have occurred thus far from a soul level. Give forgiveness, gratitude and love to everyone and everything. Even in the most tragic of circumstances. You must see through the dark to see your light shine through. God is good, my friend. God is only the light within you. The God you are so uncomfortable with is you feeling uncomfortable with yourself. You are God breathing and living. God is so very real. Look in the mirror.

How to Change the World

The only person you can control is yourself. Do not find frustration with not being able to change anything or anyone outside of yourself. That is why your focus should be on changing who you are and what you give to the world. In doing this you are changing your energy. The only thing that can change things for the positive is changing the energy you give off. The world has been a place of negativity, suffering and lack of love. We see this in historical events and times. To breed more of the same energy just makes it continue on. Like they say, violence breeds more violence. Anger breeds more anger. Anxiety breeds more anxiety. Sickness breeds more sickness. You cannot bring the same energy to a situation thinking it will stop the negativity. This is true for war and large amounts of suffering. It is ironic then that we bring more violence and power struggles to end war situations. In the end, someone wins and stops the war, but the energy put forth will only breed another situation of conflict and suffering.

This is true for something as big as a world war as well as for your personal relationships.

Past Events Breed Energy that Affects Us in the Now

Yes, the past did occur, but is the past still occurring in the now? We have pictures, video and books filled with accounts of the past. They continuously remind us of what has already happened. This can be a good thing, but this can also be a bad thing. Whatever the past is can continue to breed the same energy in the now. Can we allow the past to remain in the past? You may say yes, but most of us carry strings of attachment to what has happened to us. Why must we be reminded of suffering that took place in the past? We have movies and television shows that continually depict war, suffering, anger and horror for our own entertainment. We find entertainment in such events, but when they occur in reality we don't find it very pleasant. Then we ask why does this happen? What we think we therefore create. When we constantly view images of these types of experiences we again manifest it in reality. When you watch things that bring out fear in you, you breed fear within yourself. There are two emotions that breed like fire: love and fear. Fear paralyzes us. Love frees us. Fear prevents us from living and creating our ultimate dreams; love produces our heaven on earth.

The past can help us learn and grow but to continuously have our focus on past events can deter us from living in the now.

The past does not exist. What exists are mental thoughts attached to experiences. Our current state of awareness or this moment is all we have. When we can see every experience as an opportunity to become aware of the light that we are, nothing becomes negative. Everything then becomes enlightening. Through this awareness is where we open up the doors to our higher self and truly live the abundance we are meant to live.

Breaking the Ties that Bind

Fear has been consistently used throughout history to maintain control and gain power. Governments, rulers, religion, families, societies have used this to control people and control life. People that put fear into others are the most fearful and weak. They are so afraid of life and losing control that their mind deceives them into thinking the only way to ensure bad things do not happen is to control every aspect of it. This again is a deception. As we know, to let go of control actually gives you the most control. People and situations cannot be controlled. When you try to control life and people you actually push the good away. Where you think this is creating what you want you actually are creating the opposite effect. In reality, there is no evil, there is no Devil. The concept of evil was created out of fear. Fear is the only thing that creates things that you would consider evil. The Devil can only exist within your mind when you allow yourself to believe the Devil is real. Nothing can be real that you don't find truth in. Reality is just a perception. As there are billions of people on the earth each one is viewing reality through their own perceptions and distortions. So one's view of reality is different from another's. So whose reality is right? If we were to view heaven's thoughts on what is "right," they would tell us that there is no right or wrong. No one's definition or perception of life is correct above all others. As an integral part of the one, of universal energy, we can choose, experience and create life as we see fit. We are not meant to all live by rules or expectations. Definitely not those dogmas created by the mass collective of every human being that ever lived. We have the God-given right to choose, as we want, to experience anything and everything and to change our minds. This is true freedom.

You think you are free but are you free by the true definition? Are you free enough to not let anyone's thoughts, expectations, rules or judgments affect your choices or decisions? Are you free enough that fear does not interfere with this? When you are truly free is where you are completely fulfilled. In this place, you are at peace and living your ultimate vision of every dream and wish your heart could imagine. This is where the impossible becomes the possible.

We only categorize right and wrong because of our internal drive to fulfill our divine purpose. Every single person shares the same drive. All of our thoughts and actions are based on the drive to feel fulfilled, find happiness and know love. It comes from the soul. It does not come from the mind. So if everyone is trying to find this ultimate state, there has to be a way to find it, right? This wouldn't be considered what is right but an ultimate truth. This could also be seen as an ultimate knowing. To know the ultimate state of peace, happiness, joy and abundance. This is our true state, or better described as our true self. We go through life experiencing, searching and striving to attain this state. We are trying to find our way back to ourselves. Remembering again. We go through certain experiences that cause us to lose our self only to have the goal of finding our way back. Isn't it ironic? There are all these hurdles and obstacles that get in the way of us finding our way back. We have the initial conditioning of our mind from our family, society, the media and our environment. We have the "rights" and "wrongs" of society that we must adhere to. There are all these rules, regulations and expectations that conflict us. We have a consistent stream of fear that surrounds us on a daily basis. With all this going on we wonder why we can't obtain this ultimate state. We wonder why we are plagued with disease, depression and anxieties. We wonder why there is constant conflict within our relationships, within our society and within countries.

How do we break these ties that bind us to a way of life that prevent us from finding ourselves and therefore living our ultimate truth? Isn't that why you are reading this book? Your awareness has expanded. Your internal drive has pushed you outside of the consciousness of the masses. To find who you really are you must go where you have not been before.

Creating an Earth Where We Are One

Once we stop bringing forward the past into the now and break the ties that bind us to this past we can then create a new earth. Deep within each and every one of us we want change. Change in our individual lives and change on a global scale. Yet our mind is afraid of change. This tug of war battle continues within us and thus leaves us in limbo. In this position, no change will occur. The current state that you want to change will thus continue until we can let go of our fear. We must bring forth a new awareness of how we view ourselves, what we view life to be and what we want to experience. We are never obligated to our past. We are not obligated to anything outside ourselves. When we take on this feeling of obligation we then tie ourselves to people, to things, to situations that are not for our highest good. You purposely tie yourself to things out of fear. To prevent change people try to control people and situations. They create situations or experiences that allow them to take control and force people to feel tied to them. This then fulfills their fear but also increases this fear. Usually, the only way to get over this fear is by actually experiencing it, so the universe creates situations that allow you to feel it and have it move through you. What you express you therefore must experience, as this is the law of energy. How do you learn a lesson? You must experience an event that allows you to fully see what you are expressing or giving. To constantly feed another's fear is to enable them. Give thanks to others who allow you to learn this lesson without actually experiencing it. You can learn from others' actions by observing. This can prevent future hardship for yourself. These are gifts given to you by others.

Can we stop the progression of suffering from the current state of affairs in the world and within our own lives? The answer is always yes. There should never be a point where you accept there is no way out or that things cannot be resolved. No matter how dire the situation may seem or how deep you are involved it can always be changed for the better. This is the universal law. As much as the human race unintentionally creates its own destruction the universe will always work to move everything to a place of balance, peace and harmony. You are the reason for the current state of the world. Yes, you and each and every person on the earth. Just because you are not directly linked with certain global events or suffering, you still have a stake in creating it, even situations that occur on the other side of the world. You still played a part. You are connected to everything on the entire planet, every human, animal and plant. You hold responsibility for the happiness of another or the suffering of another. Where one person suffers, you suffer. Where one animal is tortured you are torturing yourself. Where one person's choice is taken away you will then have your choice taken at some point. It is a big web with invisible ties to each other because you are all one. One energy force, one mass, one being that has been divided. If you combined every human, every animal, everything on the planet you would be one being. This is what you call God. This is the God you all see, as the one being above all others, the ultimate creator. This is God, Buddha, Allah or any other ultimate being in any religion. The ironic part is that you are all looking to yourselves, you are praying to yourselves. You are a piece of this God and everyone around you is God. The cow in the field is God. The rock on the ground is God. The chair by your table is God. Everything that is physical is a piece of the whole. This whole being, everything on earth, in the universe and in heaven. Without one piece of this whole, there is then not a whole. So where you see someone as not worthy, not equal or not godly, you then are saying you are not worthy, not equal and not godly. When you separate one piece of this whole, it is not whole anymore.

The soul wants to be whole. It wants to be complete and connected with everything that is itself, which is everything within this mass oneness. This is the ultimate state of being and in this place you are happy, harmonious and at peace. The human race consistently separates itself from each other. In doing this you are causing the opposite of peace, love and harmony. It is okay if your mind does not find truth in this, but in your truth, you will never find peace, the ultimate love or happiness. In the opposing truth, you will continue to find yourself and others experiencing hardship, disease, natural disasters, war and conflict. If you are okay with these things then you may continue to think, live and act as you have been. Again, you are given the choice to be whom you want, to think, to act and to decide on your own free will. This is something that all of heaven and no God can ever take away from you. Even if you choose the path of disharmony, heaven will still be there loving you and seeing you for the perfection that you are. No matter what your decisions, choices, actions and beliefs are you are no less perfect, you are no less worthy. The abundance of the universe does not judge or give more to one than another. The universe gives without rules and without expectations. The universe in every moment is giving its abundance to each and every one of you. You can see this for what it is or see it as a deception. You can choose to see life as lacking and hard or you can see it as abundant and easy. All it takes is a change in your awareness and suddenly life will change. That is why every moment is a chance to change everything. With the change in your thoughts, everything changes instantly.

The next moment has not occurred yet so in the next moment anything can happen. Everything is possible. In one moment life can bring you your heaven on earth. Can this really be possible? Try it and see. We dare you.

Can you be a scion of faith and deliverance? Can you be fearless as to know that every moment that you come upon is an opportunity and that any concession of the many choices you face will bring you nothing but your ultimate happiness? When you can change your awareness to this then you will be able to immediately identify the situations that are not in your best interest and what is your higher path. As you continuously live in this new awareness the breeding of unwanted experiences will continue to decrease until every moment brings about your ultimate happiness.

Paris

Shall we walk the streets of gilded stone, lined with gold railings? Where rainbowed flowers glisten and birds sing French love songs. Life is full of romance in every corner, every sight and every experience. This thing we call romance, what is it? Why do we long for this romance? Is it a feeling or a thing? Is it something we do? The things we say? Romance is to experience beauty and love. In what we find beautiful we find romance. To love is to express this thing called romance through actions and words. Could we find romance in everyday life without the need for another to give it to us? Can we smell a flower and find that it gives us sensations that open our heart, fulfill our mind and give us emotions? It doesn't have to be another being that gives us this flower. We can ourselves find the beauty in the flower that gives us this romance we yearn for. We can hear something that makes us feel good about ourselves. The feeling of silk on the skin can be romantic. The sight of a beautiful sunset can engulf us with emotions of beauty and love. Life is filled with an abundance of sensations and yet we don't allow ourselves to fully experience these for one reason or another. It could be our religion, culture, beliefs or experiences that have built a wall around us. We are stuck in our self-contained box and we may see this on the outside but our minds deceptively tell us it is bad. Most of us even go as far as to think life is not meant to be that "sensational."

Let us dissect this word "sensational." We see the core of the word is sensation. We usually associate the word sensation with a positive thing. You feel an energy that creates a positive reaction physically. The word sensational is usually used in a context to express feelings that trigger happiness and joy. We are meant to live life through our sensations. To experience things that heighten all our senses. That is why we are here. To experience our light and love through all of our senses, to feel the ultimate sensation of love, to taste the delightful creations that our imaginations can concoct. To hear the noises of the physical all around us and to see the overwhelming beauty of the world in every corner and every face. What is the point in living if we cannot intoxicate our senses? Beauty, peace, happiness and love—these are healthy intoxicants. You can overindulge in all of these. Some people, however, reach to fulfill the holes with intoxicants like drugs, alcohol or harmful behaviors that are poison to your health and happiness or to the mental and physical safety of others. I won't dampen the beauty of our talk of Paris and romance by diving deeper into these unhealthy intoxicants, but it's a good comparison to see the spectrum of lifestyle choices.

May I exemplify the magnificence of a place so grand, so radiant, so full of life and vibrancy where life is truly abundant. It's as if we have created our own little heaven fit with gold staircases and the Garden of Eden as our personal playground. Fit with the animals and people to enjoy. May all who come to live and play be just as joyous as I as they cross the gates from mortality to the eternal. Let us all live like gods and goddesses. Let us all love with fiery passion, with abandon. Where food grows abundantly from our trees and wine flows from our fountains. We may converse with the lamb and sing in unison with the canaries. This is truly heaven. May all who are blessed to befall the earth come here to delight in all the exquisite magnificence this place may provide. Death may befall me but it shall not phase me, as I will awaken to the same place. For heaven cannot fare in comparison to this blissful realm on earth.

Once Upon a Life

There are multiple lives converging at one moment: a past, a present and a future. They all run together seamlessly, a never-ending story. Where our present actions, from the smallest kindness to the pain we cause, are thus creating our future. One day our now will be our past and the depth of the unknown before us will be our present. The now is only the outcome of our past. A circular journey. A passage through time.

I knew the moment I saw you I had been waiting for this moment all my lifetimes. All my lifetimes added up to create this moment where I would cross your path so that you would once again remind me of who I am, where I came from and the agenda of my soul. By one glance, by the sound of your voice, I realized there you were. How, I don't know, but I held a knowing that I could label as fact. That face was not new but old and comforting. Maybe we shall only pass each other by as we continue on our

100

journey, or maybe we'll once again be blessed to walk hand in hand through this life. No matter how brief our encounter may be, the taste left on my tongue will forever be remembered. I shall meet you again in another future in a world where we may have the ultimate pleasure of observing side by side the rewards of our eternal journey.

Every person and animal you may have the pleasure of knowing or of having an experience with, whether brief or long, has a contract with you. A contract to help you learn something, which we like to call remembering. Your mind is never learning something that you don't already know.

I will not give up. I will not let this be just a fleeting experience. I hold the reins. Do I give up because it is easy? Or do I follow my gut and have faith that there is a higher reason we crossed paths and our meeting was not meant to be fleeting? I think we both know but are confused by the experience around us.

Timing is key. Everything happens at the perfect time to create the best possible outcome. Change happens perfectly to bring balance back to our existence. The quicker we can become aware of what our experience is teaching us the sooner we can create a better, happier existence. Let the emotions go. You have no attachment to anyone or anything. Your happiness does not reside in someone or something. Look at the experience before you clearly. Study it without want, need or restrictions. Anything can change in the blink of an eye.

An Attachment to the Past

The past is shown to help you see the truth of the current state of affairs. When you find awareness of the why then you can change the outcome. There is a reason for what is happening. Don't think so hard. It is when you're not thinking that you see and find the answer. There you find a knowing. When you know something you don't question or think too hard. You see the chair in front of you. You know it is a chair. It is a fact because you can physically see it. Why would you analyze and think about this chair or question the chair. Do you ponder why the chair is there? No, most of us wouldn't analyze something like a chair to this extent. You just know it's a chair. Let it be a chair and let it be itself in the process of life. Naturally, your image of a person or experience is what it will be. Let it be its own image, not your interpretation of it. It could be exactly as you want it to be but the distorted image your mind creates makes it appear anything but what it really is. You are the only one keeping it from yourself. You deceive yourself into thinking it is set in stone. Your mind then won't let it be anything else, so you are the only one stopping it from manifesting.

What is not happening in front of your eyes is not a reality. Isn't this hard to grasp? What is happening in that dimension is not really happening because you are not experiencing it. The only thing that is real is what is in front of your eyes right now. What you are experiencing exactly in this moment. For example, if you are sitting in a coffee shop at this moment reading this, the only thing you can truly say is happening is what is going on in the coffee shop right in front of you. Let's say your partner is at home and not with you. Whatever is happening with your partner is not a reality as you are not there to experience it. You, for the most part, have no idea what your partner is experiencing in the same moment. Your mind could conjure up something you "think" is happening, but it is not reality. What is not happening to you in any given moment is not really happening. This may be a little hard for your mind to wrap itself around.

Anything not in your current experience does not exist except in your conceptual mind. Things continue to exist only because you make it real due to your mind imagining it. Isn't that an eye-opener! Thus, you're creating every moment. The next 15 minutes are being created now. Tomorrow has no agenda or concreteness because it has not happened. What is happening now outside of your awareness is not happening.

In the physical, you can only experience one conceptual viewpoint at a time. It is how this dimension works. In the higher dimension, you can experience multiple conceptual viewpoints at a time. You can be in two places or more at once experiencing different things. You are reminded of what you are conceptualizing. That is how thought, words and actions work. What you think, say and do is then being reminded to you in your physical experience. What you know is then shown to you to remind you of your knowing. When you can finally become aware that you don't "know" anything. Where you don't find fact in anything. This is a place where anything is possible. You don't know what your partner is doing at work right now. You don't know that it will rain tomorrow. You don't know that your marriage will last forever. This is the duality of fear. Being confident and knowing fact is the opposite of fear. Where you don't know, you usually find fear. This is only because you label time to the unknowing. Where you can let life be and evolve naturally without knowing or fearing, without comparing time you have found the key to the impossible.

Lost and Found

Nothing is lost lest our mind says it so. Everything is possible where your mind sees it so. Anything can happen instantly if the mind believes it so. Love is in every corner, in every moment if your eyes can see it. Where nothing lies it is only because your vision is blurred. A blind man does not need to see it to believe it for all he needs is his mind's eye. In this everything can be seen and experienced. It is sometimes our senses that distract us from the truth. We miss the true beauty in the experience before us. Where we can take in an experience with all our senses we truly are experiencing at the height of our soul. In this moment you are feeling true ultimate happiness. Only where you clear your deceptions and open yourself to the ultimate awareness can you live at this level of sensation. When you let fear and negative emotions take precedent you block your sensation receptors. To keep yourself chained to experiences or people that feed fear or negativity makes it difficult to cleanse your senses and experience your ultimate state of happiness.

In the current state of the world, humans spend most of their time working, caught in this vicious cycle of working to survive. There are some who find the truth and work to express and experience their ultimate happiness. This is then not work. This is then just expressing who you are which fulfills your every need and want. This is how everyone should be living life.

Life should conform to you. You shouldn't conform to life. Humans like to use the word fate, but when we rely on fate we give life the reins to our life and we just live. When we take the reins we take creative power over what we experience. Fate can be completely whatever you want it to be. Your fate can be as grand or as minute as you make it.

Nothing is lost in life. This is true if you lose an earring or if you lose a job or a relationship. Even in death, nothing can be lost. We may lose the physical body, but we are still ever-present, living and experiencing. What you know becomes fact and fact becomes reality. The most impossible ideas can become reality because someone knew it could be possible. They found fact in this knowing and then it became a reality. It is the process of the metaphysical experience we live in. A metaphysician heals and changes the physical through energy. To change the physical you must change your output of energy. To see something as found it therefore is not lost. So if you think you've lost something but know it will be found again, it will be. Again, in the mind of the universe, everything is easy. The universe does not measure the physical in any sense. It has no sense of time, money or size. Everything is easy and everything is possible. Everything is beautiful, abundant and meant for the greater good of everything in the whole of everything that ever was, ever is and ever could be.

Use this concept in your own life. It is an easy exercise that you must practice every day. Let's say you lost one of your diamond earrings. You have no idea where you could have dropped it. Something so small could be like finding a needle in a haystack. The thing is, it is somewhere and it is sitting there waiting for you to find it. In her book, "The Lightworker's Way," author Doreen Virtue divulges the perfect affirmation: "Nothing is lost in the mind of God." When you find you have lost something, state this affirmation in your mind or aloud if it helps. Say this to yourself as many times as you see fit throughout the day.

As you affirm, "Nothing is lost in the mind of God," think of the thing you lost and imagine yourself finding it. As you say this you're changing your energy to that of knowing you will find it for it is not truly lost. It will be yours again. The universal energy has no sense of time so you cannot put a time factor into the equation. You can't say it will be found in an hour or a day or a week, but you know that no matter the time it will be found. So do not get discouraged. Where you find doubt you prevent the outcome of finding the object. That is why this affirmation helps to maintain the sense of knowing mentally.

The Mirror That is Mental Illness

Mental illness is conflict between the mind and the soul. For a long time, we have seen mental illness as a sickness. Something that is beyond our control. As in getting an illness or disease. We are therefore overtaken by the genetic lottery or some ill fate to find ourselves with a physical or mental sickness.

Everything must be expressed or released. To release is to let go. Letting go of its effects, its hold. Must the human mind always find a solution or an answer to everything in life? That is what the universal energy is for. When you can let go and trust you let the universal energy take over and create a resolution for the physical. To push for something that has not happened is unnatural. Thus, you create an unnatural reaction or outcome.

This holds true for emotions as well. Feel emotions, express them and let them go. Release the hold they have on you. To internalize them is holding on to them. It's taking on the responsibility of the emotions and also the event that caused the emotions. Holding onto emotions causes a physical reaction. Everything must be expressed so even emotions must be expressed in the physical. To release them relinquishes the physical effect they will have in your experience. This will allow peace to flow through you. Everything is energy and the natural state is a constant flow. Allow emotions to flow through you. Don't attempt to hold on to them.

Mental illness is an expression of your internal emotions and thoughts of oneself or experiences that were not released. To internalize emotions or trauma is, in essence, hiding from these emotions or experiences. Again, everything must be expressed and released. You cannot run or hide from any emotion, situation or experience. The best way to create the best outcome and maintain your peace is to accept it, express your thoughts and feelings about it and let it go. Awareness is key. As human beings, we don't fully understand all the time why things happen or why hurt is caused upon us. We allow the world around us and the experiences we have to define who we are. They create this distorted vision of oneself. We often blame ourselves and see ourselves as inept and imperfect. It can ultimately cause the fear of oneself.

Most mental illness is caused by the deceptive view of oneself and this distorted self's relation to the physical world. As we always say, never find truth in the physical because it holds no truth. The physical world is just a creation of your mind. Where your mind is distorted you then create a distorted physical experience. You don't need to have a mental illness to be living in this ill-fated physical reality. Most human beings in a "normal state" still see, think, feel and act with a distorted viewpoint. This then causes an unreal experience, meaning one without truth. Every moment is created out of your prior thoughts, feelings and actions. Every moment you are creating the next moment. Your entire life has been a culmination of your mental state. The thoughts you have, the emotions you feel and how you then express these through your words and actions.

We must better understand what mental illness is. It is not an illness. It is a distorted viewpoint and a conflict between the higher self and the mind. It cannot be cured by medication. Can it be cured? Yes, it can. We must view

111

all things, people, plants, animals, illness, disease and disabilities as one. We separate them with names and definitions. We want to understand the physical differences between everything in the world so we analyze and break it apart. We separate it from us because it is different. Things we do not understand we strive to control and rid ourselves of. What is not seen as "normal" or "happiness" we work to rid ourselves of. Could we view everything in life as something that is just a part of the whole that is life that is us? Could we see disabilities as just another expression of beauty and another version of ourselves? Do we need to define something to fulfill our mind seeking resolution or a definition? We want a definition because it fulfills us in a sense that there may possibly be a cure or a way to change it. Choose to see something for the perfection that it is. Whatever *it* is, is a part of us. The part of us longing to be reconnected back to the one source energy that we are.

If we take a step back to view the bigger picture, we'd see that mental illness presents itself as a means to mend the self. The mental imbalance is due to the conflict between what the outer world appears as and our higher knowing. The physical world is the false reality whereas our higher knowing is truth or "reality."

For example, depression results from the false reality that we are separate from everything. A sense of disconnection from source or love and light. When we can find the awareness that the idea that we are all separate is false, we then find truth in the understanding that we are all connected with everyone and everything at all times. We then find connection and love within the self. This clears the illusion and brings us back to who we really are, resolving the conflict. This mends the separation between us and everyone and everything. It is the lack of awareness that causes us to find truth in the false reality around us, which is the source of our mental conflicts.

We are conditioned to believe that the physical world outside of us is "reality," but it is this belief that actually separates us from our higher self. The more you separate yourself from the higher "being" that we are, the more convoluted this physical world becomes. The more we can connect with our higher self we find that truth lies within us and that most of what appears in our physical reality is actually false. The more we realize we don't know, the more we are accepting of the infinite possibilities in the entirety of the universe. It is only those who are fully aware that find the space of peace and happiness. To open your awareness is being able to take any bit of knowledge and give it the possibility of truth. It is those who open themselves to all possible truths and find intrigue and acceptance in all beliefs or ideas that will unearth their heaven on earth. They will see that anything in this life is possible, and there isn't only one way of being or living. The more you tie yourself to one thing, one idea, one belief, one truth you will never be able to grasp peace, happiness and fulfillment. It will always be right outside your reach as these "attachments" keep you in a limited box where you then only experience that which support your attachments.

When we can find this truth in mental illness we can then change our relationship with it. Where we once viewed it as this horrible negative thing that is again this separate entity that is not us, we can now find acceptance of it and nurture this mirror of ourselves. We can view it as the child in us that is hurting. We must give it the understanding, love and acknowledgment that it is calling out for. The human mind wants to run and get rid of this "thing" that humans for so long have seen as hideous and disease-worthy. We even have labeled it as an illness. Some unforeseen fate. We take medication to numb the feelings and emotions of this mental state. We are shutting out the part of us that is crying out to be loved and nurtured. The very reason it is there is for us to experience it and understand the reasoning behind it. That which we fight and run from is what we should actually be giving love to. It arises for us to heal a part of ourselves to bring us back to balance.

The biggest challenge to overcome is to live outside the minds of everyone else around you. Nothing going on around you or to other people has anything to do with you. What appears on the outside is nothing but a mirage. A trick of the eye. They use all their energy to mask the truth on the inside. The image to them is better than facing the truth. You must step outside your comfort zone. You must face your fears. This is where peace and happiness lie. An image can be worth a thousand words, but truth is worth more than any word. For the truth cannot be placed into words. It can only be felt. Where there is truth there is peace. Where there is truth there is nothing physical. It is everything but the physical. The physical picture of peace and happiness does not appear on the outside as this. This picture may seem small and meaningless. It may not be grand or defined by human standards. It may not be filled with quantitative measure, but for those who truly know what peace is they can pick it out of a million pictures. This is because peace lies where you least expect it to be. Humans have delusionized its existence and location. We seek it out in our relationships, in physical objects, in places, in what others think we are. We seek it in the comfort of our fears.

You seek the fear, the disfigured life that others have. This is your delusional mind. You seek the things you know won't give you anything meaningful. Trust and jump into the wind of nothingness. This place of nothingness that everyone avoids is where your heaven on earth resides. So stop pining for that which is false and accept the unknown, the empty space that is the universal energy, and see what awaits you.

The Blank Script

The blank script—oh how empty, how intimidating. They
are just words yet they bring up torment. To communicate
with each other we find physical letters that in turn create
sounds to make out what our thoughts are. We use them to
indulge, to feel connected, to relay our feelings and our
experiences with another, but oh how they get us into
trouble at times. We overindulge just a tad communicating
our feelings, emotions and thoughts. Trouble awaits when
we use our emotions to communicate. There are so many
different emotions: rage, anger, sadness, obsession, love,
happiness. These emotions tend to distort the truth to our
heart. As our heart expresses love our ego and emotions
mix to paint a completely different picture. Anything
expressed that is not love and understanding is fear-based.
Your script is your life story. When you find bits of your
story or negative experiences you don't like, you can
pinpoint where the ego distorted your words. It is not

what you truly meant to communicate from your soul level. This is where your ego and fear took control and manipulated your reality. Again, where you find truth you find fact, and where you see fact you know without a doubt. This unwavering knowing is what changes your awareness and ultimately changes your outward experience. To find the awareness of your ego is to find truth in its effects. In that position, you take away its power and see the true reality of things.

You can look at your future now as an empty script, blank sheets of paper awaiting your story. You're the author of your own life. If you look to create your heaven on earth the first word on your script should be the word "love." That should be the beginning and end of your life. When your foundation is love you then create your ultimate fantasy. This is the fantasy that your soul yearns for. This is where you are fulfilled and whole. Nothing more or nothing less could make it any more perfect. Love is the answer to all your questions. We all want balance in all our relationships whether it is in our romantic relationships, our families or our friendships. How do you find a fulfilling, happy, lasting relationship? Give love. Not just to people you want to have a relationship with but to everyone in your life. This will breed love from every angle in your life.

Compare & Contrast

One aspect of life to avoid is comparing and contrasting your story with others'. This puts you in love with another's story, not your own. You already know you do not want that story. You want a story of your own. A story that is your heaven. It is the conditioning of the human mind to compare and contrast your life with another's. What another has and what you don't. People tend to see others' experiences as better than theirs. The truth of the matter is what you see is not what is the truth. As in all aspects of the physical world we have learned that we cannot always find truth in what we see because it can be deceiving. The physical is a mirage, just an image. If we strip the image away to find what is beneath we see that in reality this person's experience is grossly disfigured. A note of caution with this thought: we shouldn't always approach every person and their experience as if their image is false. We can use this concept to change your internal thought process to understand that what another has is not necessarily what we want. From the outside, you may want the relationship, career, money or house they have, but if you were to get those things they may not be exactly your "ultimate heaven," as your eyes and mind can deceive you. This can be motivation to create your own heaven whatever that may be. Don't base your heaven on another's because we all at a soul level have a different version of our heaven; we all dream differently. To let your mind or ego lead you on your dream making, you then create anything but. You must clear the mind and transcend your ego to connect with your soul's intelligence to truly find what your ultimate dreams are. When you start creating with your soul you find an experience that is enlightening, orgasmic, fulfilling and harmonious. In this state, you create a dream as well as serving others in their dream creations. This is your soul's purpose. To create its own heaven but also to help others create their heavens.

Conflicts

In most novels and movies there must always be a conflict to maintain suspense with the reader or viewer. In writing our life scripts we must remove all conflict to create our ultimate story. It is a deception to yearn for conflict. Some people in a sense search for conflict within their lives. They are not intentionally looking for conflict but their mind unconsciously creates it due to internal conflict and past conditioning. To do the same thing over and over again creates the same result as we have learned from many scientific studies. Until you are aware of this dynamic in your experience you cannot change it. To change a common theme in your life you must change your view and actions. To be mentally conflicted creates this in your outer experience. To fix the outside we must first mend the inside.

A world that is separated more and more is what you call evolution. Humans, animals, nature and the entire earth continue to separate from itself, to create many millions of different forms. To adjust to the changes, everything has to conform and take advantage of the things around it to survive. The goal of all is to maintain life and to create. Life in its natural process constantly changes to bring itself back to complete balance. Nothing can happen unless it is for the advancement back to harmony and balance. Anything not in line with harmony creates conflict. Conflict in the mind and the heart creates disharmony in your life and in the lives of everyone in the world. Again, to hate is the natural pull because it is all around you. Hate only breeds hate. Love will only breed love. It is the highest natural law that rules over the universe and the lives of all living beings and creatures.

Heaven has already told you what to do. Your soul tells you what to do. If you're having trouble hearing it it's because your mind's thoughts are getting in the way of what is reality. The fear is so loud it drowns out the truth. You already know. You know better. This is a useless conversation because you're already doing what you think you're not doing. You're doing the right thing as we speak. If you are reading these words you are already aware. You are already ahead of the game and have assisted in the change of the world. You may not know it but you alone have made the world better by working to change your individual life. To be happy is to heal others and heal mother earth. You cannot assist with others' happiness without finding your own first. You can only find pure love when you are able to give pure love because life gives the energy back to you that you are expressing. Where you find hardship in your relationships you can pinpoint the source by looking at yourself and the energy you are giving in life.

You are the master author of your own script. Here is your chance to open your dream factory and start conjuring up the most exquisite story in the history of your many lifetimes. Make this story the most memorable and you'll have your soul always coming back for more. Let your soul be reborn with the beautiful aftertaste of the best life you ever had. Oh, how your soul will shine after this.

What's Duke's Kind of Holiday

The present can be your past or the present can be something new with the beauty, class, love and abundance of the past. Whatever you choose can be yours. Why miss the past when the past can be ever present in the now? Can you create a new now? I don't think you've ever been able to use your abilities as you can right now. Never in your thousands of lifetimes have you held the knowledge and power you do right now. Thank you for being you. You are a soul, nothing more. A soul that is housed in a shell. A physical shell you call your human body. It does not define you. It is not the be-all end-all. It is but a form that assists you in your humanly journey. It is this form above all others that your soul craves to be. Cherish it. Love it. Be thankful for your physical you. Show others how abundant life can be. How magical every moment is.

Never analyze the present with the filter of the past. Most humans are conditioned by what has occurred in the past.

So they then approach the present with the emotions, feelings, reactions and fear of what happened in the past. The present is given so that you may create anew. Every second is an opportunity to change everything. A second chance is presented to us to create a new story and ultimately to create a new ending. In this opportunity, everyone or everything is then something new and different. Things only stay the same when we define them the same.

Why do Things Reoccur?

We may have situations that seem to repeatedly keep reoccurring in our lives. This could be people, relationships, situations and experiences. This can show up as good and bad. This can happen multiple times in the same life or repeat itself in different lifetimes. The things we label as "bad" only occur because we are not able to realize who we really are in the first experience. Therefore, it will continue until it helps us awaken to the truth and see who we really are. Once this realization occurs we then react differently. It is only through our reactions and choices that we continually create the same experience. If we are always expressing who we really are then we will continually create the ultimate experience of love, happiness and peace. In this instance, the repetition is favorable and seen as a "good" thing. If the experience is not so favorable, it is a sign that we are not being who we really are. This includes many things such as patience, understanding, support, help, guidance and freedom. If you combine all these things, you get pure love. People or events may present themselves as something that is "bad," but you can choose to see the truth in this false deception. We see that every person we meet and experience we have has presented itself to create our ultimate happiness. Once you realize this and approach the person or situation with pure love, the person or event then creates itself as your heaven on earth. Everything that occurs and every person you meet in your life are there to assist you with creating your heaven on earth. Everything is either made to be your heaven or it is a doorway into your heaven. If something is a doorway it is there to be your transition into your heaven. If you remain in the doorway you then are too afraid to step through the door into the place of your ultimate experience.

If you find reoccurring hardship in your life, it is time to stop and take a good hard look at who you are being. What were your actions or choices in the same experience in the past? What caused you to react in this way? You usually can pinpoint emotions that came up that caused you to react this way. For the most part, all emotions that cause us to react in a negative, rash way are due to fear. If this is the case, we did not overcome our fear but were controlled by it so much that we reacted in a way that was not pure love. Therefore, our awareness was not found. You can see awareness having a higher understanding. It is an objective view of yourself and the world around you. Through awareness, you are learning something that you didn't know before. Where we gain knowledge we become more powerful in the sense of freedom, not power as in having control. To be powerful in a spiritual sense you have control of your experience rather than life controlling you. In this state, you find happiness, peace, joy and pure love.

How should you approach the situation to create the best outcome that creates your ultimate ending? The most important thing is clearing the fear. Letting go of all fear. This includes emotions, thoughts and feelings. If this is a reoccurring situation, seeing how you reacted in the past and not replaying those reactions and thought patterns is key. Where there is no fear there is truth. Once you let go of fear your mind and heart are clear to connect with your higher self. Your higher self or your soul knows all. It knows what decisions and reactions are best in all situations to create the best outcome. Your fear causes you to make decisions that are not in line with your higher path. These decisions create hardship, conflict and suffering in your life. In a reoccurring situation, you want to approach it anew. You must let go of what happened in the past and see it new, fresh and abundant. If you approach it with the glasses of the past you define it before it can even prove its truth to you. It then ends in the same manner as it did in the past.

Decisions do not cause bad karma. It is the manner in which you play out your decisions. If you decide to leave a relationship, do it with pure love. This means be honest, understanding and patient. Relay your message with love and support and understanding of the other's feelings. Most important is to be honest. Honest with your feelings, emotions and needs. Deception is the biggest factor in causing suffering to others. No matter what the truth is, being honest is key. The soul only knows truth so where you cause another to see deception you cause conflict within the mind and soul. Conflict is the only cause to suffering. Conflict is against the natural state of all. Conflict is the only cause of anxiety, depression, stress, sickness and fear. Honesty creates the best outcome for all involved. No matter how badly you view the truth, honesty is always best and will assist you in creating the best outcome. This is the whole truth and nothing but the truth. Lies will only create an outcome that causes suffering for you and for others. If you must leave a job or relationship, you must do it with pure love. Then, if the other party still takes it badly and is suffering, it does not create bad "karma" for you. It is through their deceptive mind that they suffer.

A mind that is free and in balance will see everything for what it truly is. No matter the experience you should approach it with love and understanding. You see it for what it really is, as simply a doorway to your ultimate happiness. Knowing this you react with gratitude and love. This event was the best thing that could have happened to you as it was not meant to be your heaven and it must end to bring forth your heaven. To prolong suffering due to fear only creates more suffering. The more you prolong the truth the harder it will be. Prolonging the truth is being dishonest to yourself and to others. As your mind may see it as being selfless, it is the most selfish act. You are preventing another from their ultimate happiness all because of your fears. Your fears are the only evil in existence and they mask the truth. In truth, there is nothing to fear.

To step forth in the face of fear with honesty and love will deliver you from being touched by the things you fear the most. Happiness is not wrong. Again, your happiness brings more happiness to the earth. Revel in the beauty. Another's hurt and resentment is short-lived. It is only in you following your heart that they will find theirs. On the other hand, to control another by tying them to you due to your fears is sucking the light out of them. It is no different than theft and murder. To take another's experience to live their heaven is like taking their life. To take a life is the exact same. You are taking this experience of heaven from them. Heaven is everything and anything your soul experiences whether it is a physical experience or a higher dimensional one. Find the awareness that each experience gives you. It is through awareness that you stop the reoccurrence of "negative" experiences. We use quotation marks around words that the human mind uses to label physical experiences or people. Once you reach a higher awareness "bad," "evil" and "negative" do not exist. Everything is for your greatest good. Everything happens to bring awareness to yourself and to ultimately assist you in your higher purpose, which is to live your heavenly experience in the physical.

Life is but a short-lived lucid dream. Make the most out of your time on earth. Live each day openly, honestly, proudly, happily. Do not allow the thoughts, beliefs, judgments of others and above all your fear to prevent you from truly living your dream. Every moment is a chance for you to be who you really are. On the other side of your fears is your greatest fantasy. Today, take the first step through your fears and start truly living. This is freedom.

The Plague That Never Ends

Will you still love me when society pressures us? Will you still love me when there are others in the way? If it takes the hurt of others for us to be happy, can you do it or will the fear, the guilt and society's criticism make you cower? When you are staring happiness in the face will you turn and walk away?

We like to create an image of happiness, build this fancy yellow house, with the white picket fence. The swing on the porch and the children frolicking in the yard with the happy dog in tow. This beautiful image of happiness and perfection then changes when we look behind closed doors and find this house is filled with fear, lack, loneliness, and, truth be told, unhappiness. My little soul sits on this big earth, this beautiful, abundant earth asking why? Why are we so afraid to be happy? The very thing we search for is in actuality the one thing that scares us so that we run from it. Our minds create this deception, this false sense that this thing we call happiness doesn't exist. Our hearts and souls tell us otherwise. Our heart and soul give us our dreams and our mind smashes them. Are you fearless enough to go where you are most uncomfortable? Are you fearless enough to break through the deception your fear has created to deter you from the truth—that dreams are real and true happiness is within your grasp in every moment? The extraordinary things in life were all created by dreams. They were dreams that became reality because nothing could stand in the way of having them. Not the criticism of society, not any ounce of guilt, no fear, no obligation. Nothing could stand in the way of having anything and everything your heart could dream.

I watch by and lose hope as I see one after another sink into the abyss of their fear. They succumb to the pressure. Is there any hope that someone can stand strong and break through the fear? Can they find their authentic selves? The ideal of hope and true love. Is there another that may hold this truth in their heart? One soul worth a billion normal fearful souls. Don't dim the lights of the true at heart. They carry a light worth a trillion galaxies and we fight to dim their lights because we are afraid of their magnificence. If only we were to look in the mirror and see that the magnificence of their light is actually within ourselves, in each and every one of us. Yet the minute we see the light showing through we get scared and we intentionally darken ourselves. Why are we so afraid of the light?

To be truly happy means terror. For it's better to not taste the sweetness of heaven at all than to taste its delicacy and have it taken away. What we don't know can't hurt us, right? What we pretend is not real is again another deception we teach our minds. What our mind says is truth then talks our hearts into believing the same. We deceive our hearts into thinking love is hurt and love is inadequate. It can't be heavenly and bring happiness because that would be too good to be true. That would make life perfect, and that's just too good to be true. My heart finds another truth. That what we know of reality is actually false. That every moment can be too good to be true. This is the reality to life. That life is abundant. Life is love and happiness and everything my dreams can conjure up and more. So much more...

Fear is the only plague that envelopes the earth. Fear is the only evil in existence. Nothing evil can exist without fear. The monster under the bed was created out of the fear of the dark. The fear of expressing our natural physical desires in a healthy manner created the evil we call sexual violence and abuse. Our fear of not being perfect and moral created the idea of hell. Our fear of God created the Devil.

The fear of every single man is added to the mass consciousness of the earth and thus creates realities that are a nightmare. The Devil cannot exist if you don't believe in it. The idea of hell or the Devil only exists within your mind's eye. This fear we hide deep within ourselves and thus our physical bodies erupt with disease and thus a true plague erupts. When can we see the disillusion of the dark and embrace our light to dissolve that which has plagued us for so long?

The Four Seasons

There is a season and a reason for all. The physical world transforms itself into symbols of our internal transformative stages. We can see this in the seasons of nature. The external world must always represent the internal state within us. Therefore, the seasons change to mirror where we are and guide us on how to flow from one season to another within our lives. We are always guided by our external experience. Learn from each season and take the knowledge it holds to open our awareness and find the beauty in everything that happens to us whether we see it as good or bad. Good or bad, it is all much needed to balance us and bring us back to the source of who we really are. The cold of winter evolves into the warmth of summer. As summer tapers off nature brings out its true vibrancy of colors before slowly disappearing back into the earth. It is all a metaphor for life, death, pain and love.

The cycle of the seasons expresses the natural flow. As we go from one stage to another we see energy change and flow. Nothing stays the same. It is a never-ending journey. It can be compared to the journey of the soul. As we end one stage we begin another and so on and so forth. Once we can accept that nothing stays the same we begin accepting what presents itself in every moment or time in our lives. To be afraid of change is to be afraid of growth and advancement. Let us look more into the four seasons.

Spring

Spring celebrates the rebirth of life. What once was dead now is resurrected. From death breathes life. This is the biggest transformation shown in the physical. It is the season of birth and of creation. Life awakens from its winter slumber. The energy ignites the plants to start growing. This time symbolizes the creative energy of source. The animals see it's the time to create new life. It is a beautiful time. Feel the warmth and light again. Watch the world transform right in front of your eyes. Find the beauty in nature in this season.

Summer

At the peak of creation, we find ourselves in summer. Summer celebrates the peak of the life cycle. The earth is at its fullest. The light and warmth rule over all of life. This is abundance at its highest. This is true happiness at its brightest. We must take it all in. The warmth, the light, nature at its height of creation. This is the reason for all the seasons. It all must be to bring us to this point in our journey. All seasons are beautiful and if you analyze them deeply, you will see they are all the same. Godly, beautiful, enlightening and transformative.

Fall

As the summer wanes it carries us into fall. As the feeling of warmth fades it expresses itself in the colors it exudes. This season expresses the true significance of all the seasons. We see the true colors expressed from the other three seasons. We mentally start to slow and calm from the peak we were at in the summer. The heat cools. The days grow shorter. We can now look around to enjoy all we have created. It is the time to harvest what we sowed. This is the cusp before we go into our resting period, then moving into the stage of death. As we know, death is not an end but a rebirth. The seasons are eternal and will follow the circle of evolution continuously. The fall is truly a time for thanks and gratitude for the abundance of life and the warmth and beauty we have experienced thus far.

Winter

The last bit of warmth says farewell and the last remnants of nature fall from the trees. The light of day falls and we face the time of night. Winter expresses the beauty of death. It silences life in a layer of snow. It is a much needed time to bring calm and refreshment to the physical and to the mind. We need the cold to revitalize the senses, to remind us that the dark, cold times are just a part of the whole. We can see the beauty in this transitional period. It is just as wondrous and beautiful as the summer and spring. It is but a different experience that teaches us the many facets of dark and death. Change is needed to evolve. Death as in winter is just a transition to another form. As the leaves die off we see the true naked form of the once living, vital self. It's an indication that rest is needed. It is our chance to find the light within us to warm the physical around us. Heaven, abundance and beauty are still all around. Stop to take in the glittering landscape, the intricate composition of the snowflake and the silence within the season. This is the ultimate season to find peace.

As we travel through the year from spring to summer there is much knowledge it all brings to our awareness. Whether it's the scent of the blooming flowers of spring or the brilliant colors of the fall harvest—there is much to appreciate in everything each season brings us. We may find comfort and happiness in one season compared to another, but if you can look deeply into the soul of each season you can find the same comfort, happiness and bountiful beauty. Then as you pass from one to the next you find the change much needed for your heart and soul. Abundance is in all seasons as it is in every experience and change in your life. In this awareness, you do not let your outward physical experience affect your inner peace and balance. Every season therefore brings you peace, sensational feelings and heavenly experiences that will take your breath away.

Goodnight Moon

Saying goodnight is not a farewell. It is warm wishes for the night to come. May your night be peaceful and soothing, filled with heavenly dreams. A well-needed rest from the day's activities and thoughts. It is a rejuvenation of the mind and body.

Rest your eyes and allow your mind to drift off to a heavenly realm where your fantasies can continue. In this moment all is well. You're warm and happy hugged by moonbeams. Nothing bad can happen here. Dissolve the thoughts in your mind. Release them into the stream of yesterday and watch them fade away as the current moment takes them far beyond your awareness. Rest assured that putting too much attention on your earthly fears now would not bring you resolution. The best way to approach the rays of the rising sun is to allow yourself to drift into sleep. Goodnight my moon, my stars and my sky.

The Answers You Seek

You cannot fret away the fears of the future or solve all your problems in the now. What you actually don't realize is the solution to your problems is not in the analyzing of the issue at hand. Nor is it a calculation that you're trying to solve. The solution is in the calm and happiness within you. Where there is peace and happiness it will continue on into the future. Have faith in what is good and therein lies your answer. Your answer is right in front of you. In every moment you are seeing, hearing and knowing the ultimate answer to all of life's questions. What shall I do? Who shall I spend it with? Where do I go from here? Wherein lies the truth? Ask and you shall receive. It is as simple as that. You are living a dream where everyone around you is creating this for you. To see anything else is a deception of your mind. Everyone in the past and in the now that continues to show themselves in your life has a reason and a place to help you create a beautiful life. They give a piece of yourself back to you. They show you a world that is beautiful and fruitful. Where there is peace, love and good thoughts. Where friends rejoice and lovers comfort in each other. Where life is celebrated, food is enjoyed and drinks are shared. Where nature is preserved and resources are abundant.

Time does not exist. You know where you belong. You belong wherever you are. Here, there or everywhere. Your love is with you always. Your success is not measured but felt by your heart. Where you are breathing and being, you are successful. You have always been and always will be. You cannot receive success. Success lies in the giving. Where you are giving to another you are giving to the whole. Where you light one heart, you light a million and then a billion. Do you now see? Your success has always been and is now. Your love has been, is now and will always be. True love is the essence of being. It is not a question of who it is and when it will be. It is a question of whether you can clear your mind and see it is there and has always been there within you. Do not question. Do not search for an answer. You know the answer. It is right in front of your face. What greatness you experienced is not over. It was not taken from you. Love is your greatest gift. Give it now. You choose your ultimate love. You have the choice. In reality, there is no choice. You just know. Never doubt your heart because it is where the truth lies. The truth is all you hear. You just haven't always believed it. How can something so sweet, beautiful and loving not be the truth and not be your heaven?

You can do and have whatever you wish. You can afford your dreams. You can attract whoever and whatever you want. The universe will bring forth what is needed to make it happen. How may the universe serve you?

Let go of your past thoughts. Let go of the facts from the past that you then label as fact in the future. This doesn't allow the things to express themselves anew, in a new form or as a new experience. You don't let people express themselves new. You assume the past is still the present when the now is completely new. Everything starts new, is reborn. This moment gives life and people a chance to start over, but it can only happen when it is something new and fresh to you. See it as that. You ask for it to start over new. Well then, allow it to. It only can when you see it as new. Approach it with a fresh view without the ties of the past. Every person and situation changes minute to minute. Do not get stuck in the appearance of anything. As you know appearances are deceiving. The truth rarely fully shows itself as it is. You're afraid to remove yourself from the situation you are in yet you hate it with a passion. You want a way out but there are millions of ways right in front

143

of you. It's just up to you to make the step, the decision to remove yourself. Can this be said for another you know that is quite similar to you? Maybe they are looking for help, a hand reaching out for support, but maybe they see that the mutual feelings are not there anymore due to deceiving outward appearances. Maybe the worst is right now only due to your impatience with yourselves. Why be afraid to do anything in life? You already know you have the power and ability to make it happen. Hasn't life shown you this? Hasn't life shown you in the past that your most fearful situations turned out to be okay or even better than you imagined? Fear not. Extend the hand to support the fearful and thus clear your own mind of fear.

O'er the Land and Seas

Shall we sing of the tides and harp of the rolling hillsides?
Shall we gush of the harbors and sails of the grandest
ships? We can marinate in the warmth of the sun and gaze
at the lakes that taper off to the edge of a vast forest. Can I
forever live in the cool abundant depths and lie in the
fields of green and purple? This is happiness. This is
forever fulfilling every sense of my physical being. The
silence in the snow allows us to find the warmth within. A
needed time to quiet the mind, find awareness of the true
meaning in life. Can we truly see the beauty and
abundance o'er the land and seas?

You sit and sort through your collection of keys to find the
one that unlocks the door in front of you. You write to find
your own answers. You must write to give. We give you
your answers because the answers you seek are the
answers all seek. You find the same unhappiness that
others in life are experiencing as well. You are not alone,
my love. You are never alone. You have a fleet of angels

surrounding you. You have a family of spirits experiencing every moment with you. There are millions of people feeling the same thing you are right at this moment. People are living a life that is unfulfilling. Going to jobs they hate. They spend their time on things that bring nothing to their soul. People are lonely and want more love in their life. People have partners and spouses but they might as well be alone because they bring no pure love to each other. They take the beauty and light from each other. Heaven tells you this: You are not meant to waste your time in a position that does not bring you joy. That does nothing for your soul. That is one of the biggest problems with the world today. You create jobs out of fear and greed. The greedy run corporations that cheat their employees. They treat you like slaves. You toil most of the day for them and they pay you literally nothing. You stay there out of fear because you feel you need the money. The fear creates your reliance on anything physical, including money.

Where you are enhancing your soul and in so doing helping others, you will find the eternal abundance of the universe. Have no fear. You feel the pull to take the step that is needed. Rise above the human way of thinking and being. The material abundance will come and give you the supply needed to live your dreams and assist heaven's cause. Abundance can be manifested out of thin air. There does not need to be a source. The universe is abundant and can supply endlessly for every single living being in the world. Live then to supply others with this power, with this awareness. People's souls cry out as their minds are conflicted. Where the human mind sees lack, the divine sees an abundant oasis. Can the human mind be reconditioned to see the abundance that exists all around?

Manifesto to Myself

I will be my authentic self in every moment, true to my heart and soul's agenda. I will be grateful for every moment granted to me and not dwell on what I don't have. I understand that life happens perfectly as it shows itself. That no person or experience goes without meaning. I strive to adhere to the agenda of my soul and recognize how life advances this agenda in every moment. Life is not the cause of my hardships. It is only my fear that is to blame. To truly experience life to its fullest and receive the abundance of the universe I must open myself to my vulnerabilities and trust in life. I will not be afraid to be creative, honest and open to my ultimate potential. I will experience every moment without fear of the future or past. Nothing can be lost; nothing can hurt me because everything is for my greatest good and will provide me with everything my heart could ever want. I will love everybody and everything with passion, limitless and endless no matter who they are, what they do or say. Every moment is an opportunity for me to change everything. My intention is to serve my fellow man on behalf of heaven and to live out my soul's vision of my heaven on earth. This I vow to myself.

Manifesto to My Children

I will be true to myself. For when I'm true to myself I'm true to you. I will love you purely and freely. This means without judgments, without expectations and without selfishness. I will allow you to be who you really are. For who you are is how you were perfectly made. You are a light brighter than the stars, the sun and any galaxy. I will not force my agendas or wants on you because your soul is guiding you to experience the people and situations you need to find who you really are. I will be your angel, guiding you, loving you and protecting you. I will acknowledge your thoughts, feelings, ideas and emotions. I will live out my ultimate dreams, so that you may know how to live out yours. I will love you and everyone in life without fear. Where I am living my ultimate happiness and loving another purely I will be the example for you, so that you will find another whom you can love and who can love you as no other has in all eternity and thus you will live a life so much sweeter than heaven. May I be there with you as you experience the many sights of the world that will take your breath away. May I be there right by your side as you experience the biggest and smallest events of your life. I may not always be who you think you need me to be. I am not perfect and don't expect you to be. I cannot promise you that life will always be perfect, but I will help you to see the perfect in the imperfect. This I vow to you.

Do not fear, my child; love as deep as the universe, experience all your heart desires, let it intoxicate your senses, marinate in this experience we call the physical as it is the grandest dream you could ever imagine. Let it completely overwhelm you with the beauty it holds as it has for me. This I give to you... life in the physical.

The Sins of My Fellow Man

The sins of our fellow man are the human conditioning that causes us conflict within the mind. Conflict is the foundation of our anxiety, depression and fears. The world today is plagued by fear. Our minds run rampant with thoughts that do not serve our soul's agenda. You see anxiety is founded on a thought. A thought that has no physical form. It is not real and is just that, a thought. Sometimes fleeting, sometimes persistent, multiplying into fearful nightmares during your wakeful state. They take control of your words and actions. Anxiety is just fear of what may be. What may occur and what may not occur. You cannot find peace in a mind that is filled with constant thoughts.

I can only talk for those who want to listen and find a new awareness. I cannot speak to a person who is not truly searching for a new awareness. Those who aren't willing to open their minds to anything and everything, their self-defeating ideas and egos will not take anything from a shared discussion. Their egos build walls around them that separate them from people, abundance and fulfillment. Their ego will not let a new awareness in. For changing one's awareness is kind of like saying you have been completely wrong most of your life. This is a stab to the ego. To defend yourself you pull the ego card because the natural mind of the ego says it's everyone else's fault. It is egotistical victimization. Most of the world lives in this state, whether or not you could outwardly be seen as "egotistical." You can see when two people of this same state get together there cannot be true, fulfilling communication. It is through the awareness of the ego that we can separate the ego from our mind. The heart just wants to be heard. The human heart just wants to express and have this expression acknowledged and embraced. This is true for children and adults. There is no age discrimination. We tend to not listen to the voice of children as we feel that they are not mature enough to understand the world and their emotions and feelings.

Children are more connected with their true higher selves and thus express their emotions more openly. Emotions, ideas and thoughts are free-flowing and energy is thus felt and released naturally. As we grow up, we are then conditioned by others and our experiences to not express ourselves and to hold things in. Then as adults, the natural flow of energy is interrupted. This is what causes us physical ailments and disease. It disrupts our peace and ability to approach situations with a free mind. Where we are not living as our true higher self we cannot truly be happy and find peace. The true sense of the word "sin" is not associated with morality as defined by religion. The sin of all humankind is not living life as we are truly meant to live. It is a sin to yourself to not live your true heaven on earth. To not be able to experience and express the true abundance of the universe is the only sin in existence.

A Poem

Why write words when you can feel them? I can't truly express my thoughts and feelings in words so that you may know how I feel. I can just hold it with me. I feel a peace yet an ache. I finally realized you have always been here right by my side in every moment. Holding me, celebrating with me, watching the beauty of life next to me. I'm thankful you let me grow and learn on my own without stepping in. You allowed me to find myself. Even though I felt alone it wouldn't have mattered if you were right in front of me, because I wouldn't have seen you. I now have become aware of the irony of it all. As you did the same, a part of me was always with you. I guess that is how a soul group works. We may not physically always be together, but in reality we really truly are. We may wish it were easier and we would have found each other earlier, but I guess on a higher level we knew it wasn't time. I have written to you a lot and have received your words back. It brought me hope and calmed my heart for a moment. I enjoy the peace of my solitude, yet am overwhelmed by the life I have experienced and the beauty I have seen. I didn't settle because your fire could be felt in my heart and you soothed my restless mind. The soul and heart cannot be restless for they are whole and have everything they need to be fulfilled. It is the ego that does not feel whole and expresses the feelings of restlessness and loneliness. Humans may never be able to fully understand that our loved ones are here even though they may not be physically here. Can our mind find fulfillment with this? Our human mind wants the physicality of life. Maybe that is how we are made, as the purpose to the human reality is to feel, taste, touch, hear and see. If we didn't need this physicality then we wouldn't be here and we wouldn't be human. As we understand this concept, the flow of life continues. We are born and thus when our soul's journey is complete we then pass on to another place to continue on with a new adventure. The human mind has yet to come to terms with this. As when our loved ones die we grieve in an unhealthy manner and in many cases we allow it to destroy our state of being. This is a true travesty, and as I watch my fellow man around me grieve so deeply it brings sadness to my whole heart. What a misunderstanding that our minds deceive us with. Even though I may have some deeper understanding of this thing we call death, I still struggle with the lack of physicality. Oh, how we love the physical but how our soul finds so much more in the non-physical. Maybe it is your non-physicality that brings me this overwhelming energy of love. Others may see it as lack, but they have no idea and have never felt this. You are more real than anything physical. You are not somewhere, you are everywhere, and you are all around me in everything.

The Deceptive Mind

Help me find my wholeness, for I am whole, happy, at peace and loved. I'm the light that shines, I am the breath, I am the beauty, and I am the unknown. Why do I hurt? What do I do to move forward into a life that is fulfilling and light and that brings me peace? It's time to move away from the deception of the past and move on to the peace, happiness and joy of the current and future state. God, you listen. For I have a home, I have security. You showed me a love that is amazing. I know beyond the stars and sun that you will show me an all-encompassing life filled with fun, peace and light. I now am shown a human that is my sun and stars and I the moon. Let it be.

Can it be that a deception can be a blessing in disguise? That what is disguised as hurt is actually showing me love and happiness? It is quite ironic. Is my current hurt not real? My hurt is caused by a deception. That which is not real, or is it real? The truth always comes out. Thee who believes in truth will be shown the truth. Thee who lives in deception will be shown deception. May the truth be shown to you and may the truth clear your deceptive hurt. For does someone really love someone that they are deceptive to? Find faith in that. He who cannot let go has not moved on. He who has not moved on still loves. People deceptively try to find things to sway their attention so that their minds may not linger on the truth, the raw emotions, which are real love. Pure love is love at its rawest. For the normal mind is scared of something so pure and beautiful. That which causes the heart to sing and the soul to find peace can be the scariest thing to face.

Good Night, My Sweet

What is there to frown about? You have the world at your feet, begging for your beauty and knowledge. What tomorrow brings you will never know so make it whatever you wish it to be. You are given the things to bring forth your very own dream. Things are changing rapidly and gracefully. Take it as it is: a treasure trove of riches beyond your imagination. Things will work out, in every aspect. Have faith, my beloved, for your heart is pure. It sends the call of the light of heaven, thus bringing forth that which is pure light. Love each moment. Love each person. Do not throw away anyone or anything at the moment for you do not see the truth in the false. You see deceptively at the very things that bring you good. Don't question intentions. Don't force an outcome as you have done in the past. Let each moment be magical and let your fantasy unfold. Can you do this, my child? Can you finally allow everything to appear as it truly is in your reality? Can you let pure love come into your life and stay? Pure love magnetizes the purity in your heart and nothing or no one will stay away from you. Take them in with open arms, as does the welcoming aura of the higher realm. Be that which they cannot find in the human world. This does not mean you have to succumb to dishonesty or deceptiveness or let another take advantage of you. Beckon the flower to bloom in each and every person with love, tenderness and your presence. The flower will bloom more beautifully than you could ever imagine.

Don't Doubt, My Friend

Don't doubt. Not now. Keep the faith. Have trust and let the love in. You are absolutely right. We told you the moment of awareness brings instantaneous change. This is all good. What is being presented is nothing bad, though it may show up deceptively as loss or more turmoil. Something had to give. Something had to initiate change. To have your heaven, things must change. Believe us. Finally, you have become fully aware and in that is the change and in that is peace. This is where love lies and where true freedom is felt. You have found the ultimate freedom, my dear. In that, there is no search for answers. There is no suffering. Everything is good. Now you feel it. You embrace the bad and out comes beauty. Let things be. Don't force heaven in your experience because it would never be as sweet as the universe creating it. This is not measured on a timeline. To the universe, things transform in an instant. When you try to solve or try to force you're doing the opposite. This is resisting the very thing you're trying to create. If we have ever told you anything let it be known we know facts only. There is no deceptiveness in the eyes of the divine. As of right now in this moment you are about to be given your answers, to the now and the future if you so want them. You know it's not over. It's not meant to be over. The timeline has come to its end because it's time for all of you to live your heaven. The new awareness creates transformation, which in every form is beautiful and perfect.

Personal Trauma

What happens to us is only our past energy being expressed in the now. When we experience traumatic events it is due to what we gave in the past. You are the only one that is creating your experiences in every moment. No one else has this power over our own journey. That is why we must all accept accountability for what has occurred and what is to occur. This is not meant for us to carry guilt or anger within ourselves. It is a way to awaken to the truth, to not place blame on others, to accept that we are not victims and ultimately for us to change the future.

On a soul level, there is no differentiation between good or bad. Everything that occurs is good because it is for the greater good of our soul to grow and expand. Every moment helps us grow and become aware of our soul's higher truth. Even the most traumatic experiences occur to bring us closer to the higher dimension of love and to help us remember who we really are. When we carry the trauma with us into our future we thus create experiences that continue to make the trauma real. That prevents us from fulfilling our higher purpose and thus blocks us from living joy, happiness, peace and finding pure love. There is no way to manifest experiences that bring us true peace if we are not able to give that energy of true peace.

The only reason traumatic experiences occur is to assist our human self in finding a higher awareness of the truth. As we know, humility only occurs through experiencing things that make us humble. How can we understand the depth of darkness without going through it? It is through our own pain that we come to understand the pain of others'. If we are being our true selves at our soul level we are only expressing, thinking and acting with love. Again, life is only a mirror of ourselves. If we act in every moment with love then life can only mirror back the same. If we feel we are constantly experiencing negative people and situations then it is bringing us an awareness of ourselves. This is a sign for us to take a look in the mirror and change our way of thinking, acting and responding to life.

If we carry our trauma forward we never allow life to truly show us the beauty it houses. Where your mind is clouded with pain and hate you are not able to see through the fog.

The worse the trauma is the more we allow ourselves to hold onto it. We defend the very pain that we hate, that we wish we could eliminate. It is only by allowing ourselves to let go of the hurt that we can find our happiness and peace again. For some, letting go means pretending the past doesn't exist. If a loved one passes we want to keep them living through our pain. We may feel guilt by allowing ourselves to be happy again. It can also be a deceptive way of receiving others' love and attention. We may not consciously know we are doing this, but we must open ourselves to all possibilities.

To find your higher path you must be accepting of everything and anything. People do not want to be accountable for blame and most do not want to see themselves in a negative light. For someone to make you aware of a part of you that is not ideal you immediately become defensive. To be defensive in any situation is to be in denial. For as humans we are not perfect. That is the beauty in the physical world. It is only through the imperfect that we truly are beings of light. To acknowledge our imperfections is where we find acceptance of who we are. This is the only state that allows us to grow and change. To accept is to change. Where we will not accept change we stay in a state of denial. This state usually doesn't bode well for our soul. The soul wants to grow, but we can only grow through change.

Most humans are not in a state of spiritual nirvana. Unless you have attained this state there will always be change occurring to advance your spiritual purpose. To not allow this to happen you thus are not fulfilling your higher purpose for being in this life. When you don't fulfill your higher purpose in this life you must come back in another life to attain this individual purpose. This means you must go through the same experiences for your human self to become aware of your higher self. This experience can be seen as hard or not ideal to your human mind. Learn your lesson swiftly and gracefully so that you may experience more of your heaven on earth. Fear is the only thing that prevents you from fulfilling your higher purpose. Many a wise man has said your dreams lie outside of your comfort zone. Usually, your comfort zone is the area your fear has created. Fear likes to keep us in a small box. Our fear keeps us with people that do more harm for us than good. It keeps us in careers that do nothing for our happiness. It keeps us from living out our dreams and fantasies. It keeps us normal.

Normal is not a state to attain. We can all have extraordinary lives. We are all meant to experience this.

This is where you are fulfilling your higher purpose. You may think that we need normal people or that we need poor people and rich people. Just because a rainbow has many colors doesn't mean that we should accept that we need humans categorized all over the spectrum. The rainbow is to show you that beauty and miracles come in many forms. Everyone's heaven is a different color and is defined differently. What is the heaven your soul seeks in this life? Every life houses a different heaven for us to unearth. What color are you in this rainbow we call life?

Can we leave the trauma we have experienced in the past? The past does not exist anymore. So what has occurred is not real. It is at this juncture in your life that you must make a big decision. Don't let fear have a place in this decision. It is where fear does not reside that the best decision lies.

Why Are We All Afraid to Experience Joy?

We live by the motto "if it's too good to be true it probably is." Nothing in life can be that wonderful, amazing, happy or perfect. It's funny how we accept mediocrity and hardship as "normal," but abundance, extraordinary and bliss are deceptions. Life is that cruel, right? This oasis that we stumble across is merely a mirage in the desert. A deception in our mind due to the internal thirst for that mirage. We want to find happiness, overwhelming joy, love, generosity and people pure of heart. We love to find an amazing deal, be given free stuff, given help without expectations. This is ideal, isn't it? Is it possible to be so vulnerable, open and fearless to experience the impossible without the fear slowly creeping in? Can we stop the denial and doubt that it can be real and possibly last? It is only the fear of the deception that tricks our heart and mind into keeping our distance from that which can bring us this ultimate happiness we all internally would like. We would rather suffer than let the fear go to experience happiness. Is this not twisted? Most would say it is not twisted; it is just a fact of life. Must we always have trials and tribulations and lessons to learn? Could this possibly be our dysfunctional doing? We may not want to accept this, but what if we do? What if we accept that this gross idea of life, in fact, is not true? That we truly are perfect right now? Yes, currently, as you hold this book, you suddenly become aware that you are perfect. That the past is not real, and there is nothing more to learn. That from here on out you are here just to experience the abundance of physical life. It is not the past holding you back nor is it the fact that you still need to learn a lesson. It is only your deceptive mind holding you back. It is not your looks, your circumstances, your choices or your lack thereof. It is only your mind that holds you back. In knowing this you can suddenly change everything. A sudden change of thought changes the energy you're emitting immediately.

What is it that brings you joy and love? There is a reason this person or thing brings you joy. Don't overlook it or label it something detrimental to yourself. Once you accept your wholeness and perfection you find fulfillment in yourself. All of a sudden your happiness, peace, love and fulfillment are felt within rather than found from things outside of you. This is the ultimate state of being. Once this occurs everything on the outside will transform to bring you more of this. So this person, thing or experience will follow suit. Trust in the workings of the universe. It is the expert at creating heavens.

Energy Expressed

What is work to you? How do you spend your time? There is a reason behind everything you do. All your choices and decisions have a reason behind them. You as a human being put forth your energy and time into your work or career. Is the purpose for monetary reasons? It is because it makes you happy to be doing your work? There are many reasons depending on the individual. For most human beings you must work to maintain your survival or your lifestyle. This maintains your housing, food and entertainment. To the human mind, these are all necessities. These things keep up your happiness, your joy and your mental stability. Is this not true? Does this work you do give you light or does it deplete you? Everything in life is meant to give you more light. When it does not it is not meant to be. When something does not give you light you made the wrong decision. You took the wrong path.

As a being of light, the sole purpose of the physical life is to bring you more light and to enhance the light that you already are. Your soul is made entirely of light, which is energy. You are comprised of energy. All the molecules, protons and electrons are all energy that when put together form a physical object. That could be a human body, a chair, a car or a tree. Energy expressed creates physical objects. This can be a physical person when two human beings create life, or this can be creating an experience in your life.

Creating life is no different than creating your experiences in life. This energy creates your house, your job, people in your life and the money in your pocket. Let's look at your life, at your experience up until this moment. What have you experienced? What people are in your life? Now as we look at the physical things, the tangible things we can measure, what feelings have these things given you? The people as well as the experiences, the jobs and the money? Is this your definition of "heavenly"? Some may be described as this and some may not. Look at this all as a whole. When you put you and your entire life so far together this is what your energy has created. What you have experienced or are experiencing is your energy expressed. It is like a movie that you have manifested or

173

created from your imagination. You have manifested all your relationships, your friends and the people you come across every day. They are a direct correlation to the energy you are giving at any given time. The crazy thing is you have no idea. Humans walk around on earth blind to this fact. You can change your energy at any given time. Every moment is a new moment to change your energy, which in turn creates your experience in any given moment. Everything can change in the blink of an eye if you change your energy. Remember, energy expressed creates the physical. You are living a dream. Imagination is your tool. Your mind is your visionary tool to assist you in expressing, therefore creating everything around you. What is your heaven? Therein lies your drawing board. What you can come up with in your imagination you can then make real. Oh, the possibilities.

You can create instantly. You actually are constantly creating. It never stops. As long as you are thinking, acting and speaking you are creating something. Your dreams can happen instantly; you can manifest something physical right before your eyes. It is called a shift in consciousness. A little key to this concept is to not overthink things. Thoughts and moments are fleeting. Don't let your thoughts overtake the moment. You should enjoy every moment of your experience. When you are constantly thinking of what you don't have it overshadows the moment and what you do have in the now. The key to creation is feeling. Feel and enjoy every moment. Imagine your heaven. Feel the wondrous ecstasy that this brings you and let the wind carry it out of your mind into the beyond, into your next moment. The wind is fleeting and you do not try to contain or hold on to the wind. Hold this altruism for your dreams and thoughts. Feel them as they pass and let them fleet into the wind. See it as it is passing into the next moment to manifest into the physical and you then will step into that wondrous, fully complete and perfect fantasy, just as you made it. It is like stopping to feel the warmth of the sun on your face. In that moment you bask in it, enjoying the heat, you then are thankful for that beautiful moment and continue to enjoy the other moments that make up your experience. If you try to hold on to that warmth forever, you then miss every other beautiful moment occurring around you. Do not live in your mind. Live in what is going on around you. Feel the beauty in the moment, in the physical that is going on around you. Feel the heaven in that. Like your moment with the sun, you will find moments where you are thinking of what you would like to create next. Spend that moment in the dream you are about to create. Then you let it go. Let it be to create on its own accord. When you try too hard to control the physical and try to create it on your own you prevent it from happening. The natural energy of the universe conforms to the energy you give. It is that easy. You do not have to do anything. The more you try to control and make something happen you create the opposite. When you are calm, at ease, at peace and have that unwavering belief, which is knowing without a doubt, this is when you create instantly. To instantly have faith, without fear, causes the energy to form instantly. That's why you should enjoy what is now, because your next moment will be more than you could ever imagine. You will have moments where you think of the past and find the heaven in it, which you could not see when you were living it.

Take advantage of the now. When you can live it fully and see what wondrous beauty it holds it will transform it into something beyond your wildest dreams.

Awareness is Key

You have uncovered the essence of pure love. Do you not see the reasoning behind everything? There is a reason for all. Do not try to analyze. Don't try to find truth for it only leads to conflict. You must just believe. Now everything makes sense. Your suffering was due only to the conflict of interests and thoughts assigned to your experience. Do you not see what living in the now does to your awareness? Awareness is instantaneous. Time has no effect. When there is no fear or concept of time you are free. When you are free everything around you conforms to that freedom. When you are free nothing can touch you. You are untouchable, immortal, eternally loved and beautiful.

There are no answers, just this moment. Right here, right now. In this moment no answers are needed. Answers are only needed when you integrate time, past or future. What is needed to know about the now? Well, nothing, because in this moment, in this now everything is answered.

Everything in your physical reality is real, it is present and it is perfect. It is only the interference of thought that makes it anything else. Thought corrupts the now. It disfigures the truth and creates a false sense of reality. Do you not see that when you see the truth of the now, you realize you have everything? You have this pure love. You have this peace always. It is only your thoughts that blind you to this. You are living blindly, without sight, without awareness of the true reality.

When you are blind you use your senses to see for you. Do you not see now that your pure love has always been here? Love is not coming or something that is yet to present itself. You see the lack thereof because you use time to decipher your answers. We have tried to show you this. But the truth must be found inside yourself, not through the words of another. As soon as you understand this everything would be now. Everything has been right in front of you. You have just been living with a blindfold on and have not been able to see it right in front of you. It is not the situation that is the barrier. You have created the barrier and kept seeing it as a barrier.

Congrats to the now! And the unearthing of the being that has always been but covered, blinded by the mind and the endless corrupt thoughts. Your idea of the now or your

ultimate peace, joy and happiness did not even come close
to the reality because there was no way for you to begin to
fathom something greater. There was no way for you to
see everything in front of you with a blindfold on. You in
your mind sensed the reality by the ears, nose and taste,
but when your eyes can comprehend the immensity of the
scene in front of you, that is when the reality of now can be
fully taken in. It is not the future, it is the now. That is why
we always stress the now to you. It was always there. But
you were too blind to see. There is no fear in the now. You
know the truth to your pure love. Your happiness showed
up in shapes and forms, because that is the only way for
you to comprehend slowly what was inside of you. The
fear is only because you are looking and basing your truth
on the words of another. See, it is when you find it within
yourself that you find the comfort, completeness, the peace
and the knowingness that you are looking for. We are just
here to confirm what you already know and are. Nothing
here is something you didn't already know. It is not in the
future or the past. It is now. What is in your now? It is only
in this way that you are able to let go of the things holding
your blindfold in place. It is not in the physical. It's in the
being, not the looking. Let go of the physical and the
package that it comes in. It is deceptive. You were taught to

decipher by appearances, by the physical nature of things. This is incorrect and creates suffering and conflict within yourself.

Keep the blindfold off. That's it. Once it's off you can see the landscape before you. You can always put it back on, but why would you want to keep yourself from that beauty ever again? Don't analyze the past for answers or reasons why. We give truth in the moment. The search for truth is unreliable because the truth always changes depending on who you are. In one moment something could take a while, while in another moment it can be instantaneous. It all depends on your thoughts and energy. Truth in one moment thus changes in the next. Clear your mind of the time aspect. The more you think the more dependent you are on time and how fast things are going or not going. If you take it out of your awareness in the now the mind does not hold on to it. If you are aware that there is beauty and abundance in this moment then there is nothing to wait for.

Once you see life in this way you understand there is no journey. There is no start, no end. You create the "journey" in your mind because you interconnect life with time. When there is no time there is no journey. There is no "I need to get there" or "I don't like this spot so I'm going to try to get somewhere else." When you want to achieve you see the long road and the journey associated with it. When you let go of pleasures and desires there's nothing to attain. Love does not have to be found. You do not age because there is no journey of time. You realize the love, desire, pleasure, attainment, achievement and understanding is all inside you right now. Not yesterday or tomorrow but right now. Innocence is forever. You don't lose it. It is the conditioning of other human minds that takes this innocence away from you. You condemn the children once they are a certain age and think they must grow up for they are too old for innocence. They must mature and be responsible. What does being mature and responsible mean? You have twisted these words to suit society and as a result are corrupting the young generations. It is the young trying to regain this innocence to revive the true light inside of all mankind. It is not their lack of motivation or immaturity. They are lost because their light is fighting the conditioning of society. So what do they do? They indulge in desires and pleasures to feel good.

Once you can let go of time, you let go of suffering and any conflict in life. Truly, this is the key. Let go of the past and your mind that is stuck in the future. The past is over. It doesn't exist. It is like a dream. You awaken and it's over. It wasn't real. Every moment is fleeting. No moment is constant; it does not last or stay the same. This creates conflict and suffering whether it is a good or bad moment. It was who you were or something you did. Not who you are now. That is why they say every moment is a chance to renew, to change and to be who you really are. When you change the thought you change your awareness of everything around you and as such change everything around you. Holding on to anything means it is an attachment. You hold on to a memory or a person, place, thing or idea. This is attaching yourself to something. The more attachments you hold the heavier it weighs you down. You argue, but what are we without our memories, our beliefs, the good and bad? You say this is who you are. Who are you then? What do these good and bad memories do for you? Let's delve into that. The good you hold on to creates an attachment, which means that these good feelings, memories, people and things create a feeling of pleasure in your mind. It is like taking a drug. You take it and for a time it gives you great pleasure. You are "happy," at so-called "peace," "content," "secure," "fearless" and so forth. Correct? That is why people take drugs. It is the same with a memory or event, person, place or thing. It is not bad to have these. It is not bad to enjoy our experience called life, but when we carry it with us this makes it an attachment. It then ends up causing conflict in the mind. We then seek out more of these events, people, places and things. When we seek in any aspect we are not content in the now. We think we may be content, but if you want one of these things because it was nice and gave you pleasure or happiness, you are searching. Your mind wants more. It is a never-ending cycle. You think you want to win the lottery or you want a loving relationship or you want kids. So people get these things and feel pleasure, but the truth is something outside of yourself can only give you pleasure for a time. It is not an eternal pleasure. In your mind, you think it will but you soon realize this once the high wears away. You may be content, but you want that high, that extreme pleasure again. So you seek something else. This is how every human being lives for the most part. Just because you aren't a drug addict doesn't mean you do not fit in this category. If you want anything that is not in the now, you are an addict to pleasure. You want to achieve something, you want a better job, you want to make more money, you want more clothes, you want to find a relationship, you want to get married, you want to get a degree. You may already have something and try to maintain it even though it may not be the best thing for your soul. This is all wanting, seeking more than what is in the now. What if instead you sought nothing and simply focused on the true peace, enlightenment, true fulfillment, beauty and love that is already available to you in this very moment?

What is Happening Right Now

The purpose of these words is not to say do this or don't do that. The purpose is not to tell you what to do, what decision you should make or how you should think. The purpose is to find awareness in the now. Everything you want is all happening now. Enjoy, marinate in the now, for you have been brought to the pinnacle of everything. You have all the understanding you need now. You are who you need to be right now. You are free of thought now. The mind is free now because of the people, experiences, books and words that have been unfolding. You just couldn't grasp the whole. You grasped a part of the whole and nothing can be separated from the whole. It must be whole. It is the universal law. This has been stressed to you many times. Yes, that means everything is happening now but you couldn't see that and projected your thoughts not in this moment but in an hour, or perhaps days or months. Now means right now as you read this. You have everything right now. All the love, peace, happiness, success, stability and security you desire. If you see this now everything will transform right now. Not in an hour, not tomorrow, not in a month or a year. We don't like time any more than you. You can have all this now. It is inside you right now. You just need to be aware of this.

Why tears? Tears of pleasure or tears of the awareness of this beauty, this love. That the search, the wait, was created by you. Nothing has to wait, nothing has to grow or change because it all has and is in the now. It is so simple. Why do you even label it a situation, something that must be solved, that must be changed, a decision that needs to be made? It is only a situation where you label it one. The impossible is the most possible. Nothing is hard; nothing is too deep to get out of, nothing needs to take time. It's as simple as being aware of this. Not wanting something that isn't yours physically now. It is in the now. Does this finally all make sense? Not in thought but deeper? Do you feel it? It will overwhelm you. Not by pleasure but by the awareness of the beauty, the love, the completeness in the now that is inside of you. This moment will pass like a fleeting thought. Don't try to grasp on because you'll try forever without avail. Instead, watch with beauty and feel all the sensations it brings. Hear the sound in it. Watch it pass with delight. When you can do this the wind will forever caress your cheek. In that awareness, you'll realize the wind is trying to hang on to you instead of you chasing it and trying to grasp it. It will always be there in all its beauty and will never pass. It will just continually be. That is the awareness we speak of. The now. You have fulfillment now. Nothing you plague your mind with is real. It cannot touch you. You make it real by keeping it in your thoughts. So if you find it, the thought, don't be mad at it. Don't label it with fear. It is but a thought, a fleeting thing like the wind. Let the wind blow it into the vast eternity from where it came. If you look at it like this it no longer controls you.

Somewhere you are in your heaven. In the now you have everything somewhere. Everything you yearn for right here and now is available to you. To believe otherwise is just the mind deceiving you. You don't need to sit and ponder this or try to focus. Just know. Be aware. When you think about it too hard you turn it into something else. You don't have to dig deep. You don't have to answer anything. You don't have to picture it or manifest it in your imagination. Someone may be sitting next to you in the cafe. You don't have to ponder or analyze if it is true. It is what it is. It is real. You just know. You are aware of that person even if you aren't completely focusing on him. Correct? It's not going to change, is it? He's not going to disappear, and even though you may get up and leave he is still there. Isn't he? He is there. That is the truth. It is the same for everything. Be aware. You don't have to focus on the truth. It just is the truth. It exists, that is real. You don't have to focus on it, visualize or manifest because that is just giving the thought that it is not here. When it has always been here. The perfect relationship, the career, the eternal abundance. You just had to see it.

You have lost yourself in your life. You see yourself, but that person is not real. You're watching your life in front of you, but you've separated yourself from that life. That person only represents you. That is why everyone suffers, because your now, your reality, is missing you. Do you see this? Everyone else is waiting for you! It is not up to them to change or make decisions. That is why people around you can't make the choice to change. Everyone else is waiting for you to understand this and be aware.

You are mentally insane living inside your brain. You're in a delusional state. Everything else that has been in your reality has been there to help you become aware that you are essentially out of your mind. To completely live in your mind is to be controlled by your thoughts. We use the term "out of your mind," but technically, you are too much "in your mind." To be "out of your mind" is the place to be. It is time to see the truth and step outside the delusions. You separate yourself from your dreams because of your thoughts. This is not to imply something happening in the future because it is already happening right now. Do you understand all this? Does this make sense? You get mad when we say the now, but it is the truth. Now you see why we don't tell you of future happenings. What we tell you pertains to the energy of now. Your dreams await the day you realize this. Things change form. They transform to suit what is in your awareness. Your awareness is pure. So now your perfection is shown to you. Now you can live in the now. It has never been the future, it has always been here. It's already here. Like we said, the perfection will appear when your awareness sees it. That is the rabbit in the hat. Something can appear out of nowhere. Do not judge or condemn anything or anyone. It is not his fault. You are to blame for everything, but do not feel guilty because it is the past. Let it go like the fleeting wind. Why have we not told you this until now? Because you would not have been ready. Your awareness would not have accepted it and continued to live in its delusions. It needed to be told to you at the right moment when it was already a part of your awareness. We told you it would be overwhelming. You now have a heaven to live.

Others as well have been waiting for you. When you wait, others wait. You suffer and others suffer. You are delusional, others are delusional. You now see. This is the idea we are all one. We are all a part of the whole. You judge others and don't understand why they don't make the right choices or see the truth. Why don't they see? It is because you are delusional and you do not see. You choose to live in your delusional mind rather than be one with the whole. To be one with all beings, to live your heaven and have peace on earth in your reality. People show up just as delusional as you. It was meant to help you awaken to your own state of being. In your reality, how absurd and delusional you are really being. You judge, hate, condemn and are jealous of others. The irony of this is that you're looking at yourself because at a soul level they are you. Others are a mirror of yourself. It is time to be aware of this. It's so simple yet so complex to the human mind. Let go of these thoughts that condemn and imprison you.

You may have a decision over your head. You may be experiencing feelings of lack. Waiting for something that you currently don't have. Here is your sign. All is well and will be. The full moon acts as a marker to help signal transformation happening. Now that you are aware everything can start fresh, new, innocent, and beautiful.

Don't fear. What you feel is guilt from the past. Let go and be in the now. There is nothing to fear right now because it is perfect. Here is your reality. Like we said, everything was false. Now you see what is real. Everyone was waiting for you. Now everyone else in your life can be free. When you are free everyone around you is free. You are helping many people by being aware. Now see the global effect it has just being aware. It's all here in the now. It's not happening, it has happened. You save the earth. You save all the living creatures. NOW. Right now. You just did. Again, don't think too much about it. Now you can be free from everything. Your mind is free. Now you will see that your experience mirrors the same perfection as you. As beautiful and enlightened as you. Every person in your life is just a representation of you. That is why you should never judge because where you judge another you are only judging yourself.

You Think You Have Loved

You think you have loved. You search for love. You suffer
for love. When you can let go of desire, of pleasure, of
expectations, of its attachments, of its ideas and its image,
you go beyond it—this is love.

It is not a specific person you seek. You search, you
analyze, you squander for this someone. There is this one
and only you all want to find. To be with, to profess
promises to, to marry and have children with, to be with
for the rest of your lives. This gives you security and safety.
From what though? From loneliness, from being alone,
from not attaining the expectations of society?

We live our lives always attached to something or
someone. We are attached as children to toys, our parents.
As teenagers, we are attached to "things," clothes,
electronics, friends, to class level and relationships. As
adults, we are attached to money, things, relationships,
careers, images, identities, religions, beliefs. Do you see the

older we grow the more we are attached to? We are taught as we grow that we must be attached to more. We learn from our parents, family members and society about beliefs, religions, traditions, love and relationships. We are shown that it is the attachment that makes it real and creates the ideal image of who we are. As we grow we create more of an identity of who we are. Slowly, we create this image by all these things we attach ourselves to and by what we see others attach themselves to.

As children, we are in a pure state of being. We are pure simply because we are untouched, untainted by the image and attachments of the world. As children, we are unaware of this. It is through observation that we acquire this knowledge of attachment and of the mind's thoughts. We the world are the sole contributor to who our children become. The state of the world shows us who we are individually because we as individuals make up the collective. We are not separate from anyone or anything and until you can realize this nothing will change for yourself and especially not for the world.

We as humans seek what we lack. The soul yearns to be whole or one. To be whole you must attain what you're missing. This is the mind's perception of things. We always see ourselves as missing something, full of faults, lacking something physically or mentally. Therefore, we search for what we lack. If we are shy we seek extraversion. If we are lonely we seek a partner. If we are violent we seek non-violence. If we are depressed we seek happiness. If we are overweight we seek to lose weight. We are in a constant battle seeking the things we see that we are not or do not have. This in our mind is the process to make us whole and to fulfill this lack inside us. We focus on everything we are not. Everything our mind considers we are not is outside of ourselves. Meaning it is not who we are now. We are not happy now; happiness is not a part of our experience. We then must attain it. It is an ideal image of who we think we need to become. Ultimately, we have an image of who we are to be, which is created by the distorted world around us, by our families, environments, friends, society, religions, culture and beliefs. That is why most of the world feels empty and unfulfilled. It is this image that is our worst enemy. We are our own worst enemy. Not the world, not our family and friends, not strangers, not our jobs, our bosses, our relationships. These all condition this image, but we hold the control. We hold that deceptive image and seek to attain it. The question is can anyone really attain this ultimate image of oneself? It is like saying if I won the lottery I would be happy and fulfilled. This is a deception of the mind. It is understanding that the search is a never-ending battle. The more you search the more you find things to search for. As long as you let the mind accept the search it will automatically want to search. Meaning you can never fulfill the mind in its search for fulfillment. Fulfillment isn't something you attain but something you must be. To be is to receive. If you cannot be so shall you never receive. When you are aware, you are free. To be free of something you must be aware of the truth.

Purity we see in babies and children. We as humans see it as a fact that as we grow we lose that sense of purity. That purity is left for the innocent. Who are the innocent? Children? People who are chaste? Who defines who is pure and innocent? Can we always no matter what maintain this sense of purity and innocence in our minds? Religions state that if we follow a life of desires and lust we are no longer pure. If we don't follow the standards and rules of society we are not pure and innocent or moral. What is morality or pureness anyways? This definition can change depending on the culture, religion or our geography. So can we say that people created this word "morality" and the idea of pureness and innocence in their minds? Yes, these are all ideas created by the mind's thoughts.

It is again that search for the fulfillment of an image. It is the image created by individuals of who they think they should be and what others should be. This image is to attain complete happiness, peace and joy. So the image is the attainment of complete fulfillment. This image was magnified by the masses, which grew to be the image of the collective. So essentially, it was put in everyone's minds that this is the way to live, this is the way to attain all that we search for. So because one person decided that this was their image and this is correct we now all think alike. You may argue against this; that we are not all alike. We are individuals and we differ from that of our neighbor. We differ in culture, in societal class, education, religion, beliefs and geographical area. If you look at the world as a whole, as a collective, we can see the mind of the individual. The collective is a direct representation of each and every one of us, no matter the differential details. The world is in a state of chaos. The world as a whole is in a deep hole trying to dig its way out. Yet the very things we do to free ourselves ironically digs a deeper hole. It is the same for the individual. For you, for your child, your friend and society. We see our own lives are in a deep, dark hole and we are searching for a way out. We search for answers, things, people that can lift us out of our despair. Yet the very search, the very way of thinking is just doing the opposite. You keep falling deeper in your hole and are wondering why? The light keeps getting farther and farther away. So you keep digging. You keep thinking the same way, doing the same things hoping that something changes. Hoping, that is a strong word that we like to hold on to. A wise man once told me we must let go of hope. In hoping we are only seeing what we don't already have. In letting go of hope we can then start fresh and new in every moment. Then we are that and have that which we were hoping for.

If you dissect the word hope you will find the truth in the false, which it carries. Hope is a word the world chants. It is a word held with much authority and power. We hold on to this in our minds. It gives us a sense of safety, this word hope. We hold on to it and we feel secure. In our darkness, it gives us a sense of light. Do you see I use the word sense? It does not change everything from dark into light, but it gives us a visual, an escape from the darkness we are in at the moment. In that moment we see we are in the dark, so we idealize that there is hope for a tomorrow that doesn't contain darkness. A tomorrow where we are fearless, happy. Where we are fulfilled, joyous, abundant. A future in which we have what we lack in this moment. Hope is future tense. It is not something that is now, because if it were now, you wouldn't need hope, would you? If you were that now or had that now what would there be to hope for, correct? So in essence, you are projecting that which you are not now or do not have now into the future. If something is in the future it is never in the now. Do you understand? When I first was told this I took it negatively as you may have yourself. Let go of hope? If I let go of hope then you're pretty much saying it will never happen. When I finally understood the truth to this and didn't see the false in this statement I was able to let go of hope instantly. I had what I wished for already and didn't realize it because I was too focused on the hope, which was seeing the lack in the moment.

Could you possibly let go of the image you have of yourself, of your relationships, your children and your society? Could you fathom the thought that you held no rules, no ideals and no image of anything or anyone? In letting go of this image there are no expectations; there are no need or wants. Do you understand this? When there are no expectations of oneself or of others, when there is no need or want of anything there is just you and this moment. In this moment without any of these things or thoughts, there is just the beauty in the moment. This is complete and pure emptiness. At this level of pure emptiness, this is where you find a peace in the mind and heart. This is an

incomprehensible peace beyond description. When you
are one with the moment with no thoughts, no wants,
needs, expectations or judgments you then see what pure
beauty is, you see what ultimate peace and happiness is.
This is where you start experiencing pure love. Not with
anyone or anything but just the energy, the sensation of
pure love within yourself. This is being in balance with
your mind, heart, environment and everything around you.

People spend so much time and effort trying to be
something they are not. Trying to control everything and
everyone. Trying to attain things or people. Trying to
maintain an image one has of oneself or that others have of
them. Trying to change, trying to achieve, always seeking.
Constantly trying to solve something. Worrying, worrying,
worrying, thus suffering, suffering, suffering. The chatter in
the mind never ends. Your thoughts are constant. Do you
find that there is never a moment where there isn't chatter
going on in your mind? Do you feel like the only way to
find peace is to get outside of your own mind? You want to
have a break from yourself but you don't know how to do
this. It drives you crazy trying to solve this dilemma. So
you seek out doctors, therapists, people, objects and
escapes. You take medications. Does this little pill fix the
problem? We all know the pill is not the fix. If you stop

taking the medications you revert back to the chatter in your mind, the anxiety, the depression. You find yourself facing the image in the mirror, which is you. You face the lack you see, the imperfections and the emptiness. You are given your feelings, your emotions, mind, thoughts, heart, senses, hands and body to experience the magnificence of this experience called life. Yet you run from all these things. You numb yourself because you don't want to feel, you don't want to think, you don't want to face the truth. The truth is you. You don't want to face yourself and all the emptiness, the unhappiness, the emotions that are inside your mind. I say mind because that is what is telling you that you are empty, that you're unhappy, that you are not whole, that you are not perfect. This is all a delusion. You are whole because you are you. The good, the bad, the ugly and the beautiful. You are complete, secure, and perfect in every aspect just being this sum of everything that is you.

You are never empty or alone. The human mind thinks I'm alone because I do not have things or people, relationships. You only feel alone because you are not one with yourself. The only relationship you need to be full, to be fulfilled, to be abundant is with yourself. When you are one with yourself you find you don't need anything or anyone to feel fulfilled, complete, happy or at peace. At this level, you never feel alone or empty. You do not feel heartache. This is dissolving all attachment to anything or anyone. No attachment to an image, to an ideal, to obligation, to being something you are not. This is where you free yourself, and when you free yourself from the bondage of attachments you free everyone around you. Attachment is not needed to love or to receive love. Attachment is a need, a want, expectations, rules, images and ideals. This is the main cause of the conflicts in our minds. Where there is conflict there is hardship and suffering. When you have conflict in your mind, you give conflict to the people around you. You are causing hardship and suffering for your relationships, family, friends and everyone you come in contact with. Do you now see that when you free yourself from these chains, you free everyone around you from these chains as well? This is where you transform your life. This is where you change the world. The best way to change the world or to help is to first transform yourself and let go of the chaos in your mind. Now you see how attachment is not love. Attachments are not needed to maintain relationships. Attachments create the opposite of love. When you love without attachment, without need, want, judgments or fear this is where you find pure love. Pure love has no image. The images we use to define love are false and create that false image in the minds of all the people in the world. We

201

idealize this image and expect this from our relationships. We search out this image. When the image is threatened, when our relationships don't provide this attainment of our image, it creates conflict within our mind. This leads to hardship and suffering in ourselves and in our relationships.

Attachments cause us to go into relationships and stay in relationships that are not for our greatest good. If you are with someone because they are your source of happiness, peace, your sense of security, or out of obligation the relationship is based solely on attachment. These relationships feed your delusional mind. They do not rid you of the emptiness inside yourself. They do not give you true security. They assist you in the escape of your emptiness and lack of security. They create the false sense of who you are. You then feed the world with the false image of love. You show your children a false truth. The pureness of a child's mind is grossly tainted by this falsity, by this delusion. Their mind is conflicted by the truth in their heart, which is the pureness of love and the image they are seeing in the physical. This conflict leads to hardship and suffering as they grow. This confliction leads to anxiety, depression, insecurity, frustration and a false image of oneself and of others. They grow attached to people and things, which feeds this confliction. No wonder our world is filled with mental illnesses, diseases, heartache, chaos and anger. Anger is created by conflict within the mind. The mind is fighting with the truth in the heart and the mind's false delusions. Anger is the mind's unhealthy way of expressing love mixed with frustration. If we are ever to define the loss of innocence this is it. We are not immoral or impure because of our actions or thoughts. These are only caused by the disillusion of the truth. Is there a way to maintain this pureness, this innocence always no matter your age? The answer is yes. You do not maintain this by your images, actions, thoughts, beliefs or religions. You find this pureness within yourself when you can find the place within yourself that is free of all these things. When you can live each moment with a sense of freshness and vitality. When you can approach each moment with newness free of attachment, fear, expectations, free of the past. This is where you find this pureness and innocence. Every moment is then beautiful, perfect, freeing, exciting.

Your child is born. You have this being. This pure new breathing life. We are born with all the knowledge, the truth and this pure love within us. They look to you, to the world to assist them in this maintenance of this innocence. They know only this pure love that they brought with them from the higher realm. Their minds are not filled with chatter. Thoughts are fleeting, more like an awareness of what is happening in the moment. They are observing, not analyzing, not solving, not trying. Every moment is fleeting and they approach everything with a sense of freshness. Their attachment is solely for the basic necessities to maintain life. To eat and to sleep. Life does not flourish without love. It is not that they seek love, or are attached to the ideal of love. It is the basic instinct of the being to give love and flourish by the love they are given. Babies and young children mimic the people around them. They form attachments based on the attachments of the caregivers. Their functions, actions, words and thoughts are mirrors of the parents. Conflict in the minds of the parents is expressed through the children. How do we show and teach our children pure love, ultimate peace and happiness if we ourselves have no sense of what it is? In our own minds, we are conflicted, anxious, unhappy and empty. We want to show our children to be pure love, to be free of attachments, to not hold an image of oneself, yet this is who we are. The only way to give this to our children is to be this. You cannot show someone something you are not. Who you are and your thoughts are energy. You can try to act the part, but you cannot fool an adult let alone a child. To be is to transform, not only in action and in words but in who you are. When you are free of the mind and have ultimate peace and happiness, when you are pure love, that is when you are being. Your being is this. This is when everything around you is transformed, your life, your relationships, your children and you. How do we transform the world? One child at a time.

Soul Mates

We are put with the people and situations that mirror our internal self. Let it be known this is meant to remind you of your growth and who you want to be. Everyone attracts like-minded people. You may see differences but the energy expressed is the same. People come at the perfect time to remind you of the light within yourself. To remind you of the aspects of yourself where you are lacking or where you are abundant. Indecisiveness brings indecisiveness. Light breeds light. Love reminds us of the love within ourselves.

Someone else's soul mate may be your soul mate. You may be someone's soul mate where another is your soul mate. Life is all one big decision. Why we choose to spend our experience with one or another is all based on the agenda of the soul. The soul will guide you in the best direction that will be of most advantage to your soul. To live your highest dream is to clear the soul of karmic ties that cause us to experience a sense of suffering and lack. Let go of the fear that does not allow you to make decisions that will bring you to your ultimate goal. Nothing else is holding you back. You create the invisible wall that you see as a barrier or obstacle to get there. There is no obstacle, there is no barrier, as you are the sole creator.

All people in our life are soul mates, ties that expand through many lifetimes. They are there to show you and remind you of who you are. Their presence reminds you of the love and the soul connection you share. Soul mates are mirrors of each other. Your life was meant to unfold as such to help you and your soul mates become aware of a deeper part of yourselves.

There is No Big Secret

There is no big secret. There is no grand equation to solve. This is not a lifelong journey that must be taken to learn something you don't already know. Why wait is the question? Why wait till tomorrow or ten years from now or even in the next life? What you don't have now, you won't have in the next life. What you have now you carry into the future. If you are waiting for something then you will continue to wait. It is only when the mind decides to have it instantly will it be. So why wait. Would you rather have it now or later? This is how the whole creation idea works. Don't get stuck in the human thought about creating something. That is what keeps us in the vicious cycle of the mind. If you choose you can continue wanting more. This whole idea of acquiring property or possessions creates the conflict. When you label something as "mine" you are already setting yourself up for defeat and suffering. We as humans are aware that we all want freedom. Freedom of speech, freedom to choose, to be, to work. Freedom is sought after by all people no matter the culture, religion, society or geographic region. This is the natural state of the soul. This is love. Freedom is the essence of everything that is. It is peace, happiness, joy and ultimate love. Therefore, when we attach ourselves to something or someone, is that love? Does possessing something give that thing/person freedom? When we have expectations, does that give another person the freedom to be? If you are expected to be something you are not or if you are given rules on how to live, what to do and how to be, is that freedom? Where there is no freedom there is no real love. Do you do this to your relationships, your wife, husband, children, friends, family and employees? Why does the mind automatically think and act in this manner? Let us investigate this. This is the way human beings have thought and existed for millennia. How can we find the root cause to change the conditioning of the mind? When we do this with a goal in mind whether it is to change your life, to gain something or to find something, we are already creating conflict. This conflict taints the truth and brings the mind back to the conflicted way of thinking, which causes pain and suffering. To truly, instantly change this pattern you must be one with all emotions and feelings. We separate ourselves from the feelings we are having.

Let's say you have anger. You take that anger and see it as separate. That it is not you. It is bad and you want to not have the anger or be angry. So in thinking like this, you are separating this anger from you. It is not you. This internal fight creates conflict in your mind. The conflict is because the anger is you. It is not separate. When you attempt to separate a part of you from the whole you struggle. So the essence of you is confused. Anger is caused by a fight within yourself. You are fighting with yourself. You cannot separate anything from the whole. Yet as humans we are constantly fighting to get rid of our faults. The situation or person you are taking the anger out on is just you being angry at yourself.

Remember, every person and situation in your life is a mirror of yourself. When you find something you don't like it is something you do not like with yourself. Until you can accept the whole you and love the whole, you will find these faults in another or situation. How do you really accept and love the whole you? When you can understand that you as a whole are created in the likeness of perfection. The physical, the psychological, the personality, the feelings, the emotions are all in the likeness of one. As we look at dualities, the polarities in life—the dark and light, the hot and cold, the love and hate, the war and peace—we see that life cannot exist without both. The duality creates one. It creates balance. Without one of the dualities, there would not be balance. There would only be half of the whole.

This is the same for you. You are whole as you are. The anger, the jealousy, the anxiety, the sadness, the mental disorders are a part of the one. Then why do you fight these feelings? They don't feel good, correct? They cause you to suffer yet the very act of trying to rid yourself of them creates your suffering. That is the thing creating the suffering. Not the actual anger or the envy. It is the fight to not feel the anger which causes the suffering. The anger is you. You are not separate. You might fight this notion because you think it taints the image you want for yourself. You don't want to be labeled as an angry person. But this process of feeling your anger is not you saying you are an angry person. This isn't you being labeled as anything. This is not you creating the image of being angry. This is you being aware that the anger is part of the beauty that is you. It stems from the love within yourself. It is part of the duality. You can have the love without the hate. Accept the anger. Feel it. To find the root you must be in the anger. Can you just feel the anger without having thoughts about it? As you are sitting with this anger you see it as it truly is. It is just an emotion. When there is no thought attached, all of a sudden the emotion fades away and you are left with understanding and compassion for the emotion. That's when this anger that controls you now dissolves back into the emptiness from where it came and again you can see your wholeness.

Your mind likes to label emotions, to judge them. It's like when you see something beautiful you immediately start having thoughts. You see it and say, "Oh, this is beautiful. This makes me feel good." Then when you walk away you continue to think about the beautiful sight or person you just saw. Then you think that you want to see or feel it again. Then you compare all other people and situations to it. Right there it starts the conflict in the mind. When you compare people and situations you create conflict, which causes you to suffer. So can you see a beautiful sunset and just feel the essence of the beauty without thinking or having any thoughts about it. In that moment you look at a sunset, feel the warmth, the love, observe the colors without thinking in your head "that's purple and that's red" and compare it to something in your memory or think of another person or thing that gave you the same feelings. This is the same thing you can do with the emotion you have. The goal is not to rid yourself of certain feelings or emotions. People tend to think they are not perfect because they have these feelings. They have anxiety, anger and envy and want to rid themselves of it. You go to great lengths to find a cure. You take medications; you go to doctors, therapists, gurus and your holy priests, even God to help you rid yourself of all these bad aspects, thoughts and feelings. I use the word bad lightly. Humans label them as bad. From a human perspective, the highest image of oneself is to not have any of these faulty aspects. The image of someone holy or pure in the religious sense is to be free of all these. When we are one we have balance. When the mind is balanced you find peace. Balance can only be found when you are one with everything, including emotions that make you uncomfortable. Awareness is key. To be aware that the anxiety is just as much a part of you as the love is brings peace. What you observe you think is outside yourself. Is the thing you are observing separate, or is it really you that you are observing? Now we know that feelings and emotions are not separate; they are actually you. The people and the situations in your life are actually you so you are in essence observing yourself in every person, situation, and experience. It is all a mirror. It is as if you walk around your entire life staring in a mirror. Could we investigate this together? Take the time to see both sides to this idea. Not to immediately say you agree or disagree but to observe this thought. Could everything around you really be there to show you who you really are at any moment? Any experience, any situation and every relationship you have. We are always trying to find who we really are, but how can we be aware of this? Our experience is there to remind us who we are being at every moment. What you are being and thinking is translated in the physical before you.

Every person in your life, your wife/husband, your parents, children, friends are going to mirror who you are in the moment. They are solely there to remind you of who you are being. If you are not being who you really are they are there to show you that so you become aware. It's like you are walking to a destination. All of a sudden there is someone on your path there that tells you you're going the wrong way, you must go right to get to the place you want to go. You won't continue to go the way you were going because you know it is not right. You then immediately go right. See, I use the word immediately. You don't say okay I will turn right tomorrow or I will turn right in a year. You immediately turn right. Why would you not? If you turn right tomorrow you are wasting time. If you turn right immediately you immediately are on the right track. Imagine then if you wait a year to turn right? Life is always guiding you. So if you want to wait till the next lifetime that

There is No Big Secret

is your choice. If you want to change your next life do it now. Do it now! Do it immediately.

There is no time but now. Time only exists because the human mind created it. Time does not exist. The now only exists. What you are now the future will be the same. If you are lacking now then the future is lacking. If you are waiting for something you will continue to wait. If you wait for your true love you will always wait for this. You may find someone but they will not be that true love. The physical world will always mirror that which you are in the moment. If you wait this person you find will only mirror that. So even though you have someone they will not suffice and you will wait to have your true love in the future. Does this seem complicated? Does this bring feelings of frustration? You may think, "I could have had this five years ago but I've been lost. What a waste." Nothing is a waste. When time does not exist there is no feeling of frustration concerning time. It does not matter how old you are or what you have done all the years you have lived. The wondrous thing about the now is that it is immediate. If you are immediately aware you immediately have that. There is no wait involved. The physical world around you immediately transforms to your awareness. The mirror doesn't wait to catch up. The mirror is always there. If you color your hair blue and look in the mirror it is instant. Observe your relationship or the situation you are in. Observe the feelings you have about it. Don't attach thoughts or past memories to it. Just feel what it gives you. What are you being? If something is frustrating you, what is it about this person or situation that is frustrating? What is it that this person or situation is showing me about myself? The answers you find are then making you aware of who you're being. At this point of awareness, everything changes.

Awareness is the key to immediate change. Awareness is the first and biggest step. Don't fight this awareness. Find the root cause inside you. Embrace it. Do not push it away or try to not be something you are. Once you try to not be that or try to be the opposite you create conflict. Just be aware of being aware. There is no big change you must make. Do not focus on the future result or goal. Again, the focus is on the now. If you are not drinking now you are not drinking in the future. Focus on the moment. Relish in what you are doing or being right now. That is the key to change. This is especially true for habitual actions or ways of thinking. If you are not partaking in your habit in this moment you are successful. Do not base success on a timeline. When you involve time in anything you create conflict. Alcoholics or drug addicts are proud because they have been sober for a certain amount of days, months or years. If you are not doing drugs now or drinking now you are successful and should be proud. You will more than likely fail if you involve time in anything. I will work to make my marriage better. If you instantly are being a better person your marriage is instantly better. If you instantly want a result you must instantly change. If you know now this relationship is not your ultimate happiness, don't wait five years to see or do something about it. If you instantly are being who you are, everything around you will mirror this. Change no matter what form it takes is good.

You are perfect in every moment no matter what. No matter the anger, the actions or words you use. Love every part of your mind, feelings, emotions, actions and words. That means have no regret, no guilt. Don't put yourself down. When you accept every part of you, even your past actions, the mirror will show this. People around you will mirror how you feel about yourself. You are in control always. No one controls you or your situation. And remember, everything is immediate.

The Investigation Into the Self

Here is a little activity for you. Find a mirror. Look at yourself in the mirror. Ask yourself a couple questions. Who are you? Who are you being? Not the stats or the physical characteristics. Let's investigate you and me. Let us look deep. We don't want to just brush the surface. We want to see what's at the depths of who you are. What makes you tick. How you view yourself. What image you have created for yourself because the image of yourself is the image you hold for others as well.

To do this you have to let go of all your attachments, insecurities, fears. You must let go of your beliefs, your religion, your dogmas, your image of yourself and of society. You must let go of your traditions, what others have told you is right and wrong. You must let go of the good and evils of life. Let go of your judgments, your expectations. Let go of the past and the future. Let's just be in this moment. At this point in our discussion, tomorrow doesn't exist. Tomorrow may never come. As humans, we know that nothing is secure. We don't know if we will live till tomorrow. The past is over. We have no expectations of where this is going or that you need a certain result or a change. This is purely a conversation between you and me. Can you open our mind to the possibility of anything? We don't need to conclude whether something is right or wrong or whether you accept something or don't. We are not trying to be something or come off as this higher vision of ourselves or what we want others to see us as. I'm not here to get you to believe what I think is correct or to think that I'm better or know more than you. Only you can investigate the truth for yourself. The only way to free yourself from fear, anxieties and mental hardships is to free the mind of thought. The box we live in is our prison. When we eliminate the box the possibilities are endless. That is complete freedom. Our religions, our beliefs, our judgments, our images of society and ourselves create a box around us. They are what imprison us in this box. Do you not see?

We are freeing ourselves of thought because thought is only the mind in movement. Movement in relation to the past and the future. Thought is the mind measuring the movement of time. If we can completely let go of the past and have no expectations of the future we just have this moment. Without the comparison of the past and the expectation of the future in this moment we are truly free of the thoughts that poison this moment. When we can live in this moment without comparison or thought we find how perfect and beautiful this moment is. That is innocence. To approach every moment freely. It is only our thoughts that taint our experience.

You cannot control anything outside of yourself. People, situations, circumstances. These are all out of your control. The more you try to control the more out of control you really are. The less you try to control the more control you are in. The only control you hold is who you are and your thoughts/reactions to things. This is how you mirror your outside world to your inner being. It is the law of energy. Who you are being will be mirrored in your physical experience. That is the key to complete freedom. Nothing else besides yourself can free you from anxiety, depression, unhappiness, loneliness, anger and so on. No person, no guru, no doctor, no pill, no therapist, no religion, no priest, no place, no job. No one has control over you but you. As long as you search for something outside yourself to bring you peace, joy, happiness or love, so shall the search continue. So shall the emptiness within yourself reside and so shall the discontentment and unfulfillment.

We were made whole, one with everything in the universe. There is nothing that exists that is not within us. We are just not aware of this. We are love, we are happiness. We are the anger, the anxiety and the hurt. We are the good and the bad. You cannot have one without the other. It is the law of dualities or polarities. With night comes day. Love is fear as much as fear is love. There cannot be a north without a south. How would we know what cold is without hot? All these embody a whole. Completeness. A balance. This is also true for the being. To be complete, fulfilled and at peace, you must be one with all that is you. So we must embrace the good parts of ourselves as well as the faults. The anger, the anxiety, the impatience, the selfishness, the guilt, the envy, the greed and so on. We are told we must love ourselves before we can be truly loved. Most of us think we do, but do we really? Do you really love the kindness you give as well as the extreme anxiety you have? Now, really ponder that question. Do you embrace the anxiety or do you search to change that anxiety? Do you try constantly to escape those feelings of anxiety? Do you take pills to numb those feelings? Do you fight with the anxiety? Is it a constant struggle? So the answer would be, no, you do not really love all of you. The anxiety is part of the whole which is you. So in essence, you separate the anxiety from yourself because you see it as not who you are. It is labeled as bad. When something is not you, you strive to not be that or change it. In this separation, you are not whole anymore. So you feel unhappy and incomplete, unfulfilled. You have hardship and search to find peace, happiness and fulfillment. Only when you are whole and in balance will you find the peace, happiness, joy and love. Where you separate yourself you cannot be whole. When you can stop trying to change or rid yourself of "the bad" is when you will find you don't have the anxiety or the depression or the anger. This is where you are fulfilled. So can you see where nothing but yourself can bring you peace, fulfillment, happiness and pure love? This is being free of thought, because anger, greed, anxiety are all just thought in relation to time. Once you are free of thought you are free of these things. Then they just combine; melt together with the love and peace that you are to create a whole. This whole is perfection. Where you are free, you free everyone and everything around you. Your anxieties, fears, anger, frustrations and expectations are all chains you place on your family, friends and relationships. So you see that the chains you carry you place on the people you love as well as everyone you come into contact with. When you are not free, no one is free. Your unhappiness creates others' unhappiness.

Your anxiety creates anxiety for others. Your fears make others afraid. Can you see where all this spreads and spreads? This doesn't just affect you. It affects the people we love and everyone around us. Then the cycle continues. They spread to the people they know and so on and we wonder why the world is in the state it is in. You and I are all the cause to the state of the world. The suffering, the hardships, the increase in mental illnesses, the increase in physical ailments and diseases. Our mental state affects our physical state. When you are at peace, when you are in a state of happiness the physical—your body, mind and physical experience—can only mirror that.

If you want to change your life, if you want to know what peace and happiness are, if you are unhappy, if you are depressed or anxiety prone, if you are plagued with physical ailments and disease—you must look in the mirror. Do not look at your spouse or partner. Do not point the finger at your family or friends. Do not look at your job or your physical belongings, what you have or don't have. We blame what we eat. We blame our genes. We blame our environment. We blame each other. Human beings must always find a source to blame. There has to be an answer to our toils and troubles and it's never us. It's hard to look in the mirror and accept that maybe we are the only ones to blame. Can you open the possibility that we are the source of all our suffering and hardships? You must look in the mirror. What is staring back at you? It is you. It is your face. It represents you physically as well as the entirety that makes you who you are. You are a physical representation of everything that is perfection. Don't look to a definition of perfection. Perfection is deciphered differently depending on the observer. What is perfection? Is it something that is beautiful? But what is beauty? Can we really define what real beauty is? Perfection in its true definition is something that is whole. As we discussed earlier, the whole of everything is just that, everything. Peace is balance. It is a balance, an equal part of everything. For example, think of a scale. If you have more of one thing than another the scale does not balance. So when you have more of one thing it empowers the other. This is a true representation of the human being. From conception we are whole. We are made whole from the start, but when you don't have a balance of everything it creates an imbalance. We can only find peace where there is a complete balance of the whole. So you see, it is when you have more of something like anxiety, let's say, it overpowers the good. Therefore, we are controlled by that anxiety. If you try to rid yourself of the anxiety, you also create an imbalance. The anxiety is as much a part of the whole as the love. It is part of the whole. So when we try to cut out a part of the whole we do not have a whole anymore. So there is no balance and where there is no balance there is no peace. When we accept the bad as we accept the good, we find it does not control us anymore.

The Investigation into the Self II

You have now been given the new awareness that you are
perfect. Perfect right now just as you are, and the irony to
it all is you have always been perfect from the moment you
came into this world. Nothing has changed. You have not
changed. The only thing that has changed over the years is
your perception of yourself and who you are. Slowly, due
to your life experiences, circumstances and the many
relationships you've had, your view of yourself has eroded.
Notice, I said your *view* has eroded, not that you as a
person are not perfect anymore. Your perception is not
perfect. It is because you have let things outside yourself
affect your perception. If you walked through life and let
no one and no experience affect you physically, mentally or
emotionally, you would have the same perception of
yourself as when you were born. This is the perception
that you are whole and perfect. That is the truth. You
spend thousands of dollars going to a therapist so that they
can pick you apart. You say that "this is wrong with me"

and "that is wrong with me." You ask them to "fix me." Again, the irony to it all is that you have never been broken. There is nothing wrong with you! Isn't that frustrating? How simple is that? There is nothing wrong with you and there never has been. It is your awareness that is distorted. Until you can truly be aware that you are perfect just the way you are, faults and all, can you truly transform.

Fear

Fear is what is causing a reaction in you. There is nothing to fear. For the love you have found is all yours. Yes, hold it, love it, give it care, give it attention, and observe its beauty. Fear is what is causing you to want, judge and condemn it. It is only through awareness that you find freedom from it.

Awareness comes in many forms. Your awareness comes in love, where others' is filtered through fear. The filter distorts the truth. To correct this distortion, there must be a first step, and that is realizing that what has been cannot continue. The soul wants to love purely and freely. The dirt must be washed away to reveal what is beneath. You are the one clearing the dirt. Let what is be what it is. See the truth in the false. Allow people the freedom and the space to become aware. Do not smother or force their growth and awareness. They must feel free to find the truth in the false on their own accord. Your sense of security feels threatened due to people's words or actions or lack thereof. So to feel secure people must do what their mind thinks they need to do to make them feel good. This is not who you are. Your security does not depend on others' words and actions, for they don't prove anything. It is fact that you are the truth to another's deceptive world. It is all fact. So let go of the fear that tells you this is not true. The truth is fact. The false is just that, the false. It is not true and never will be. Remember, you have everything you need now.

Nothing is Separate

Nothing is separate from us. Not even the person next to you or your friend, wife, husband or the stranger you pass on the street. Even the dog, cat, lion, tree or cloud is not separate from you. The image of the cloud can be described by descriptive words based on its physical characteristics and the relative properties it has with other matter. It is the same with humans. You have an image of what you think of yourself and what others think of you. You tend to regard this image with high importance because this makes you who you are in your own mind. You base a lot of your beliefs on this image. What you view as right and wrong or what is good and bad for you. How do you redeem yourself in the eyes of others by your image? So you compare your image to others. If there is another's image you like better you want to take that image on. You get envious and jealous of another's image. Your image then becomes your prison or confinement. This image creates your hurt, sorrow and suffering on many levels. You are hurt or upset when someone does something you don't want him or her to do. If they say something you don't like. If their actions are not in accordance with what your expectations are. Most of our hurt comes from actions and words of others. How we are in relationship with others is directly represented in our reality.

Our experience is only a mirror of who we really are. Every relationship we have is also a mirror helping us see who we really are. They are teaching us how we have been and how we are. We are in essence observing the observer or observing ourselves through our experience. When we are aware that we are the only ones causing our own hurt we can become whole with the world around us. When we are not aware, we are separating ourselves from our experience and everything in it. This separation leads to conflict, which causes hurt and suffering. We blame our hurt and suffering on others. We must own the blame for our own experience because we created it. The more we separate ourselves the more separate our experience becomes. This experience is there to help us see this so that we may become whole once again with ourselves and everything and everyone around us. We must become aware of the reality to our experience. This is the truth in the false. Putting the blame on others is seeing the false because the truth is it is not them to blame, it is yourself. When we can see the oneness we share with everybody we then become one with everybody in our experience. That is when transformation takes place. This is where hurt no longer exists.

So now let's touch on the aspect of image. The image is the cause of our hurt. When we can see what our image of ourselves is, we can then observe the truth happening. When someone does or says something we don't like we are hurt. This is because the image of ourselves is threatened, causing fear, which brings on the feelings of being hurt. Then the hurt causes us to react or use our actions and words to protect the image that is being threatened. It is the natural instinct to protect and defend yourself, but this is caused only by the conditioning of the mind. Your mind has been conditioned with this defensive instinct. As we see though this causes us pain and suffering. There is no logical reasoning behind this conditioning. This creates separation in the mind and in our reality. If you can view yourself with no imagery you cannot be hurt by words or actions of another. This is securing the fact that you are whole already no matter what, and with this wholeness there is no need to feel threatened. We see that the actions and words of others are just their defensiveness against their image being threatened. It is just a vicious cycle of hurt and suffering due to our own deceptive minds.

The physical has nothing to do with the results you seek. It is but a shell. If the inside is not in line with the outside your reality will prove that.

Now, be clear of the truth before you. If your resulting reality is not in line with your heart, you must merge the separations within yourself and make it whole. Do you understand this? That means take away the deception of your mind. What is before you is not bad. Clear the cycle of hurt. Do not hurt and you will not hurt others. Your hurt is only due to the fact that there is separation occurring between you and your experience. You are one with everything. Therefore, jealousy and comparison is not necessary. There is no difference. There is nothing to compare. You are all linked. There is a correlation between you and everything that is in your awareness. Therefore, to be jealous is to be jealous of yourself. You do not see that the thing you are jealous of you already have inside yourself. You hold the key to this. This is you being represented in the physical. If you have no image then there is nothing to compare. Nothing affects you because the thing in front of you is you. As soon as you can be aware of this that exact thing you see will be transformed. Your reality will transform to fit your inner being. If you are at peace, if you are aware, if you see yourself as whole, as beauty and love and you give pure love this will be mimicked in your reality. This is abundance, love, success, completeness, peace, joy and happiness. You must be this before you can create this. You cannot create pure love unless you can be this first.

Your energy is matter. Your energy and thought create your reality. Matter relative to matter. The matter inside you creates the matter outside in the physical. The goal is not to create something you are not. It is to be what you already are now. Everyone houses this inside them. They must clear the illusion to find this truth. To see the truth within the false inside your mind. Again, this goes back to the now. Right now is the time. Right now is when your experience will be transformed. It is right now. You have the abundance, success, love, joy, peace and happiness inside you. You have the power to create. To be matter and light. How do you choose to use this? It is quite simple. There is no timeframe. There is no journey. It does not take time to be. Matter is instant. There is not a moment where creation is not happening. You create the journey and you also create the mountain. There doesn't have to be a climb. It doesn't have to be work. It doesn't take a lot of energy. There is no doubt where there is complete awareness of the truth in the false. It is your thoughts getting in the way if there is any doubt, fear, anxiety, hurt or stress. It is as easy as the breeze. The breeze flows easily, softly. It continues, fleeting, as is every moment. Every moment is a chance to change everything. As soon as you are aware and see the truth, everything will conform to this and everything instantly transforms.

It is Time

It is time. It is now. You have been made aware of these words. This knowledge has been put into your hands. You shouldn't doubt anymore. If there is any doubt, you are seeing the false in the false. There is no wait. You are there now. Drop your defenses. Drop the old image of who you were. This was just an image. There is no hurt. Your hurt is a defense, because what is truly being threatened here? Nothing. That image is false. A building that does not exist cannot be knocked down or harmed. Impatience and fear is the only thing in your way

Zenmaticism

Zenmaticism: To be of clear mind and judgment pertaining to the moment at hand. Which is clear of any past or future pressure or influence.

Zenmatic: A person who is of clear mind and judgment in every moment. Who does not allow the past or future pressure or influence to have any affect in the now.

As we view our own definition of "Zen" we see the real aspects of this state of being. People often use meditation to bring themselves to a state of "Zen." To meditate is to clear your mind of all thought, of the world around you. At times we use a visual to focus on in order to rid ourselves of all other thought. In this place you are still "thinking" and there is still thought going on because you're using one thought to distract your mind from another thought. We are not saying this is bad or good. We are just dissecting this term meditation. Even though it may not be the intention, meditation is a way to escape the normal day to day workings of the mind and our normal thought process. Escape the agendas, the work, the things we must do, the stressors, fears and anxieties. The mind is trained to quiet itself, to find that sense of peace that most have no idea of what it feels like. People only think monks can live in a state of Zen in every moment, but if you watch them they meditate for long periods of time. As we see in our definition, being Zen is not defined as being a Buddhist monk. Zen is a state of mind clear from thought. It is our thought that creates anything but peace and happiness. Thought is just a by-product of the mind.

Time does not exist. It only exists in relation to the human mind trying to make sense of experience. To rationalize or lay expectation to a series of events. We think time is needed. Time is needed to grow something, to be something, to attain. Work must be timed. We work a set amount of hours, years, months. Success can be measured by time. Work, relationships, a marriage's success factor is measured on time. Same with school. You must go to school a certain number of years to get a degree and to fulfill an expectation of society. What is the meaning of this degree? It shows you are knowledgeable in a specified field or area. You are an expert when you complete a certain number of years. Individuals with PhD's are experts more than someone with a bachelor's or a master's degree.

To understand this concept we must look into the definition of an expert. An expert is someone who knows a certain topic or subject better than others. Meaning they know every angle, the what, where, when and why. In most cases, experts know how to fix something. They can help you understand something, which others do not. How do you measure someone's expertise? After we have spent much time researching, studying, and experiencing something? A person with a PhD now can be called an expert on love, disease and even life events. To search for anything is a dead end path. To seek an expert to fix your problems is a never-ending cycle. We want an expert to somehow prove to us that they are an expert on a certain subject or situation. A degree, a piece of paper can prove this to us, but can something prove to us who this person is at their core? Are they a being that is such an expert that they are able to be that which they teach. Are they one with this thing or subject? An expert on love and relationships: Are they pure love? Do they know what pure love feels like? How can we know what another's truth is? There are no rules on love or relationships yet we spread this to others. The experts know how to fix people's relationships or life issues. We as humans seek out a source to fix us, to fix our problems, to cure us of our dysfunctions. What is the cause of all our dysfunctions and problems? Could it be a conflict within oneself?

I am not claiming to be an expert. I am not here to tell you I can fix you or change your life. These are thoughts within the mind; thoughts that I have and that others can ponder. A discussion that you and I can have together, as one, on the same level and plane. Just two beings with no image, no separation between us. A group of light beings searching for understanding and searching to change our lives. We are one in each other's likeness. When we can let go of our own images of ourselves, let go of our beliefs, our traditions, cultures, rules and expectations, then we are on the same page together. Here we are one. We can then communicate in a way that is beyond the depths of society and human minds. At this place, we can discover and be one with everything. This is where we are being who we really are. This is where we are free. At this place, we then realize love, peace and happiness is not something that we find because it has always been inside us. This is pure love.

Can we love like this as well as communicate like this? The question is not whether this is possible but whether you can be this. You have been conditioned your entire life to not be this. Your society presses this. The media portrays a skewed vision of love and of how we must be. Our religions boast love but increase the conflict. Everything creates the conflict within us.

Forget the human rules. Forget the sensible observation. You can't use the normal rules for every situation. Any sense of trying to control someone or something is creating the opposite reaction of what you seek. The ironic thing is what you seek you already have and are. So allow that pure love to release the last of its ties to the false. It is only pure love that can totally free attachments and ties. There is no sense of time. Time does not exist. Things are created instantly. There is no sense of time or growing in the universe. You have something or you don't. You're doing something or you're not. You're being that or you're not. That is why there is no winning or losing. In a pure mind, there is no sense of this. In every moment you have everything. In that state, there is nothing to win because you have it all and nothing to lose because it does not exist. The release of false attachments is just another beautiful thing because it is giving you your ultimate happiness and love. You know all you need to know. The answers are all there. What you see is not false and it is everything your heart tells you is real. There is no falsity in this so there is nothing to fear. Your ultimate heaven is exactly what it appears to be. If you question or tie society's rules to it you are tainting the beauty of it. Words are just that—words. Judgments are just that, judgments, which are the mind creating rules to an internal conflict. Don't let the conflict of others ruin the beauty that you created. When you are living your dream others only judge and hate due to the conflict within themselves. They want the dream and when they see you in your purity attaining this they want what they don't have. Everyone can have and live their dream if they let go of the things that prevent them from having it. They won't sacrifice the image and rules they have been conditioned with. Your dream lies in the place where your fear does not allow you to go. Don't think you haven't been creating your dream. You have already created it. To compare it to anything, to see a lack is false. All that's left are the tiny details that will appear instantly. To my fellow Zenmatics, Zen on, my friends.

A Tale to Heighten Your Senses Part 2

We haven't met in a while. Welcome back. Since we met last the story stagnated a bit but there is still so much to take in even if life seems to stand still. The story continues to unfold. For us the best story is where we find peace, harmony and above all love, lots of love but the story of all stories isn't easy. The greatest of all loves is found by breaking through the greatest of obstacles. We don't understand your fears, your preconceived notions and truthfully the drama does not suit our tastes. The drama at times may be the only thing that opens you up so you can connect back to who you really are. You must experience what you are not to know what you are. It's the same with finding what you don't want, to then create what you do want. Life is a series of people, places and experiences to help us find just that. To stay where we don't want or continue to be what we know we are not is against the whole reason you are here. We are just flowers waiting to bloom. The light, the water tends to us, nurtures us until just the right moment. Don't judge the process or try to speed it up. Life knows perfection, trust it.

There is so much yet so little for us to relay. In the human mind there is always so much you want to know. From a divine perspective there is nothing to ponder or question. There is nothing to know as all is known. There is nothing to fear because all is and will always be well. Love is all there is and in this moment there is nothing more or less than this moment. There is no past or present as they are all converging at this same moment. Everything is divine, magical and brings balance to the essence that is you. We tend to speak in pictures because doesn't a picture speak a thousand words? Instead of draining energy on finding words to represent a thought or feeling we relay a knowing. There is no point to get across, because there is nothing we need or expect. We just are. When you just are there is nothing you need from another to experience all that is. When there are no expectations there are no conditions. When there are no expectations there is nothing that can cause you suffering. Do you see that the people and experiences you have had are helping you become more aware of all this? They are not there to cause you suffering. It is all a great picture providing you everything you need. As long as there are conditions to your happiness there will be suffering. As the human mind cannot lay forth a path detail by detail that will provide the ultimate dream. It is only the higher essence of you that has the map. Let go of the effort. Isn't that grand? You can just lay back and enjoy the ride, while the universe figures out the plans and details. It's like enjoying a story that you didn't have to write. Then when action is required you will just know and take the right action that will bring you to your next heavenly experience. This is the path of your greatest joy, which is one of ease and grace.

Sorry to go off topic, but back to the story. Oh, where did we leave off? Oh, yes the ethereal half dead being. So much has occurred. The sacrifice of her dead half did not end there. What she did not realize is that she became the sacrificial lamb. She must sacrifice all that is physical to reemerge from the ashes as the phoenix, the light that she really is. Divinity is only realized by letting go of all the false conditionings of the human mind. This was her souls mission to become all that is source to then radiate this light unto the earth to help others awaken to the light that they are. She traveled and searched every corner of the globe for all that was beautiful. The sites, the people and experiences slowly awoken her, filled her with light, wiped her tears, healed her wounds, infused her with new blood.

Along this journey her twin was always there, watching, waiting, supporting her. His soul was thought to have been killed off but can you ever really kill that which is immortal? I think not. Out of his love he died for her because he knew she would never be that which she was meant if he had always been there. So, he sacrificed her to all that is, he loved her and than he hurt her. He murdered her light, he bloodied her soul but he did it all out of his eternal love for her. What they didn't know is she sacrificed herself for them both. When she thought he was dead. When she thought it was the end. She had no idea. She now stands here in this moment. In the height of her light. When she could not find more. When the beauty of this earth filled her every cell. When she was whole once again. When she accomplished more than she could have ever imagined.

The moon stands above her swollen, full, reigning in the night sky. The warm air caresses her as she walks a dark path. Now the horrors and fears of the night now became her comfort and security. She no longer fears the dark yet revels in it. For the mysteries within the dark reveal the greatest treasures. The trees watch as she passes. They sway ever so gently to signal to her. Speaking their words of wisdom. Sending their love. She just was. She wasn't trying or wanting. She just was. She was one with the vast forest, the expanse of darkness and the eternity of the sky and beyond. When in a clearing ahead the moon illuminates the path before her and there stands a figure. The figure did not frighten her but intrigued her. She stayed back to watch from afar. She does not want to frighten him as he seems lost. She knew the dark and the beauty it holds. He seemed different and she was pulled to him. She slowly approaches him and as the light of the moon hits her face he gasps.

What she doesn't know is he does not gasp from horror he gasps as her physicality in that moment ignites, love, beauty, peace, desire and fear all at the same time within him. Isn't it ironic how all that is divine when experienced in the physical ignites fear within the human mind? He stood in this moment not sure how he got here. Memory lost. Face to face with all that is his heaven yet all that he could ever feared. Quite a conundrum. What he doesn't know is their stories are intertwined. He is because of her and all he did was for her. Who she is and this meeting is for him to find who he really is and write the story of all stories.

She reaches out her hand and he steps back. He knew if he grabbed her hand it was over. He could never go back to what was. He looked behind himself and saw only darkness. As he looked behind her he saw the unknown. He may be willing to follow the dark path ahead if she will light the path but will she always be there to light the path or will she disappear into the fog leaving him in the darkness to find his way back alone? But back to what? More darkness? He's spinning. Nothing makes sense anymore. Is this just a deception leading him to his demise? As the siren calls the sailor, as the goddess seduces the mortal. Could his mortal self of flesh and bone be able to live amongst this ethereal figure? Could he become immortal or is the true deception in the mind of the physical? Were we all deceived to believe folklore as tale or was it all real? That all that was immortal and heavenly was truly meant for us to experience. Were we all just conditioned to fear to prevent us from finding our power and realizing that Mount Olympus does exist and we are all actual gods and goddesses? That is if we believe and let go of our false human conditionings. Above all let go of the fear. Heaven is reaching out its hand to us at many points in our life. Will we grab the hand that will take us to our heaven on earth? Maybe it's not the hand of someone outside of us. Maybe it's our selves reaching out to guide us back to who we really are. You lost your way let me help you back to where you belong. Let me show you the way as I was lost myself and paved the path. If it is really ourselves then can we really ever lose that which we are? Overthink much? What he doesn't know is he has a much higher purpose than he could ever imagine and the universe waits for him to grab the hand that will lead him to his throne.

She stood calm, strong and patient. She traveled the same road and saw herself in him. She understood. She would not run or hide. She questioned this series of events and wasn't quite sure where the story would go next but learned to trust all that crossed her path. In this moment nothing could be more real and clear. She was gentle and did not force but stayed with him in the light of the moon. It was not a bad place to be. She enjoyed his presence and even though all she wanted to do was come closer and make out the definition of his face, feel her hand in his, memorize his physicality, she didn't want to scare him. She knew what was to come. For to have the two of them at the same moment want the same thing would be even sweeter.

For her it all comes together instantly and she recognizes him. It is her twin. The twin she thought she lost forever. The dead half that was killed off. How has the universe brought him back from the dead? The universe has intertwined their paths again but he is in a new form.

Everything she never knew she always wanted. The recognition leaves her frozen, stunned.

It was meant to happen this way. It is the universe conspiring, laying out the greatest of divine stories. So where do they go from here? Just wait the best is yet to come...........

Pony

A Pony as is the Unicorn is a mythical creature born of our imagination. Is our imagination creating that which is fictional or is the imagination in truth our higher self-guiding us to what is truly possible? We dream of that which connects us back to our deepest fantasies, fills us with bliss and intrigue. It takes us out of the mundane world that humanity has created for us. It brings us to landscapes and realms that our childhood mind could see and be very much a part of. The innocent mind allows itself to open to the impossible. To be excited, to create, to allow the self to just be. This is a divine creature that shows itself to those that believe. Proving that you are the magician and magic is all around. Do not mistake this unicorn as an illusion. A unicorn is very much real. You cannot capture a unicorn or force it to come to you. A unicorn will come to you when you are aligned with its divine frequency. As you express the love within your heart the unicorn will appear before you from out of nowhere. You can't connect with them with the words and tactics of the masses. Call to them in truth and love. For they reside in an etheric paradise and are guiding you back to your true self, your true nature. To live forever in this paradise you must release the fear, the hurt, the guilt, and the false conditionings of society. The frequency of love and bliss they encompass may trigger your deepest fears but it is only in the darkness surfacing that you can heal and release it forever. For those that have been blessed to have crossed the path of a being of such…..the truth is you are one as well. For the unicorn can only be attracted to that which is like itself.

In you I found a mirror of myself and through your eyes I saw who I really was and for the first time fell in love with myself. You ignited something in me that expanded me beyond this earthly reality. In this I awakened to truth. The truth that love and bliss do not lay in another or outside of us but is within us. It is because of you I have uncovered my heaven on earth. For love cannot be defined by our human programming. Love is unconditional. Love shows up unexpectedly and awakens you to someone you never knew was always there. Hiding beneath all the false conditionings of what we were told love is and how it should look. I don't love you because of what you give me or what we have. I love because you just are. Our connection is that of the strongest magnets in the universe. Pure love challenges you to become the greatest version of yourself. It brings up all the darkness within you so that you can release it and become the light that you were always meant to be. Others may not understand what we have but it's what everyone wants in the deepest depths of their hearts.

What Have You Given to Your Fellow Man?

Can we ponder a moment together? When you are faced with the end of this life, what will be the final question you are left with? What meaning can I take with me? What will bring more light to my soul as I pass from one world to another? It all comes down to one question. What have you given to your fellow man? As you exit this physical world, say goodbye to your current existence, the person you knew yourself to be, and walk into the light of perfection. Look back upon the existence you led, the experience you created, the choices you made. When you are free of fear, of doubt, of wants, of attachments, your soul is completely free and clear. In this space, there is no sense of time. Time does not exist in the non-physical world. You gain a sense of clarity that you never had before. You now understand the reason for it all. You see what you should have done and how you should have been. It all seems so easy now in this moment. In this new world you are in. Even though you see the mistakes you made, what you left in the world, there is no sense of guilt.

My friend, what did you give to the world and your fellow man? We're not talking in terms of material things or of success, but what feelings, memories and love did you leave behind?

Ask yourself this: Did I give love to my fellow man?

Did I leave the world with more love and peace because I was there?

Did I bring people peace, love and light?

Did I live unselfishly?

Did I give more than I received?

Did I give anger, hate, envy, sadness, guilt, pain, stress and judgments, or did I give love, acceptance, forgiveness, understanding, freedom and joy?

There are a lot of questions here. Why are there more questions than answers you ask? You can only find true answers within yourself. No one else can give you the answers you seek. Someone can give you their answers, but can most people really find truth in the words of another? For most human beings the answer is no. Truth again comes from experiencing something or finding proof.

In physically experiencing something or someone showing you evidence or proof you then label this as truth. This is real, tangible, it is right, and you find a definite answer. If you truly want to know you shall find. If you ask, you shall receive. As you ask honest questions with true integrity you shall get the answers. Life will give you your answers. The truth inside yourself, which is the part of you that is all-knowing, will give you the right answers. This is not your mind, this is your soul. For as you know, your mind is a deceptive machine and we should never lead with our head. If you get truth from your mind you will be led astray. This is where you make mistakes. When your mind is deceived it causes you to make decisions based on emotions, which are in turn mistaken for your heart. Emotions and the heart are two different things. Emotions are vital to the whole experience of life, but they are not there to assist in the choices you make.

Love is an emotion but true love is free of all emotional ties. Does that make sense? True love is not the emotion. You think you love someone, but do you really love them or is it an emotional tie? Is this love based on an attachment? Is your love fulfilling your need for security and safety? What if you then take this love away? What are you left with? A sense of incompleteness, a feeling of insecurity and fear. This is true for any love attachment. Love between two human beings. Your love for your religion or faith. Your love for success or material possessions. Your love for your culture and traditions. If your love creates an attachment it is not love. You know if you're attached if your sense of well-being, stability or sense of who you are is based on this love. Love does not create fear, judgments or expectations and surely does not create anger or harm toward another. If your love for someone or something creates this it is unhealthy and is solely based on the attachment you have. If you take away someone's love or someone's religion or someone's culture it can cause great fear within the self. You attach who you are to this thing or person. So when someone or something else threatens this sense of you, your love for another, your faith or religion, you feel fear and lash out with anger, defensiveness and judgments that can ultimately lead to mental or physical harm to another. This is displayed by an individual and then spreads to a whole group of people displaying this. What are these individuals or masses of people giving to their fellow man? What have they left the world with? In the end, when they pass and find themselves standing in review of the life they led, what will they find that they gave to other human beings and the world? They caused sadness, anger, pain, confusion, separation and above all fear. They were oblivious to anyone but themselves. In the end, we realize what we give is ultimately what we get back. You cause your own pain, disease, physical ailments, fear, suffering and hardships. You do this all in the name of your faith, religions, cultures, traditions, for the people you love, your attachments, all due to your fear. When it's all said and done you must experience all that you left behind, all that you gave you must therefore get. If you created separation between yourself and your family, friends, between cultures, races, religions you will have to be separated. Why you ask? To understand the separation. When you are then experiencing it, you realize that this is not who you are and not what you want to experience. It is the whole duality of life. How do you find empathy and humility until you are on the receiving end of the suffering? Thee who causes suffering does not know the pain he causes until he himself has suffered. For to experience the pain is to find humility. To truly understand the light we are we must also see the darkness. What is the point of light if we don't have the dark?

What is the lesson of this chapter? Become aware of why you're really here. It is all about assisting your fellow man in achieving their higher purpose and spreading the light that you are. Then as you are looking back on your life you will be able to experience the love you left behind.

The Root of All Suffering

The lack thereof, therein do we find sentiment.

Time, thought and comparison is the root of all suffering.

Thought is based on our past and our analysis of the future. Thought is nothing more. So thought is essentially movement through time. We create time due to thoughts in comparison to the now. Again, time is nothing more than the movement and measurement of thought. We have an experience in this moment and then we have another in the next. So the first experience is then recorded in the mind as a memory and labeled as the past. The thought of something tomorrow is the future.

What is time comprised of? The past, the present and the future. We invented the clock to measure time passing. In essence, we are measuring thought. When we attach time to thought or measure thought we create conflict within the mind. So then to measure is to compare. We are constantly measuring or comparing the past to the now.

You remember a bad memory or a good memory in association to what is currently happening. In that, you are reliving that past memory. You are either yearning to relive an experience again or are fighting to not re-create a certain experience from the past. The thought is pulled from the past into the now. Thus creating thought about the future. The thoughts we have of the future are nothing more than the projection of our current thoughts. These current thoughts are the confliction between the future and the past. So there you are stuck in a vicious cycle of constantly comparing and reliving past memories. What you are thinking in the now is then creating your future. What you have in the future is the same as what you had in the past. What you have today you have tomorrow. Unless the cycle stops, the future can only be that which is now.

The key is not to stop anything. There is nothing to fight, to prevent, to stop or to start. In the awareness of the cycle is where it ceases. Can you be aware of something without thinking about it? Can you observe without assigning any thoughts to it? Remember, thought is only our memories and beliefs, which are all based on the past. To be free of thought is to be free of the self or the "me," which is only an image that was created by the collective of all humans throughout history. When you are confronted with nature there is only the present. Envision yourself on a beach, viewing the vast ocean, the sky, the sand and all its vast colors. In the intensity of that moment, all thought stops. Where you are experiencing with your senses and not your thoughts you then can truly experience this beauty. At that moment the self ceases to exist because there is no thought of how you are looking at that moment. You are not thinking of the email you didn't send, your wife, kids, the lawn you have to mow, your obligations. This is where you are truly experiencing the now. You are living in the moment.

Can you observe your emotions and feelings in the same way? Can you just be in the moment with your feelings? You feel loneliness creep up. You feel anxious. This is due to overthinking. Your thoughts work to escape the anxiety or loneliness. Anxiety is not something you want to feel. So you fight it, you try to escape it and try to rid yourself of it.

Nothing real comes from thought. Truth, happiness, creativity and love will never flower from thought. These only come from the place where thought does not exist. Therefore, to find answers, to find love, happiness or truth in thought or thinking is false. No truth can come from thought. So to find truth regarding the answers you seek, you must be free of thought. Outside of thought is absolute knowing. In that absolute knowing is the absolute truth. In absolute truth is your ultimate happiness, peace and joy. That is where you will know real love.

Can We See the Truth in the False

I'd like to go over the concept of what we find as true and false. Can we clear our minds and open ourselves up to anything and everything? As we communicate together can we be open to the possibility that anything is possible? That what we have always known to be true may truly be false? Can you entertain this possibility, as it is the only way to truly see the truth in the false and the false in the false? The things you hold on to with a death grip—your religion, beliefs, cultures, morals and views on life—have all been false. So the truth you find in this reality is really not the absolute truth. Seeing the truth in the false is truly being able to see the truth in a false reality. It is like looking at a picture and focusing the eye to find there is another picture within the picture.

Can the mind truly let go of all its desires, attachments, beliefs, traditions and cultures? Can this thought even be entertained? Is there a possibility that you may be able to actually free your mind from the chains that bond you to your suffering and internal conflicts? We are not going to say that this is definite and that you must do this to get rid of suffering, pain and conflict and to find peace, happiness, joy and love. Just let your mind ponder this. Maybe allow yourself to say, "It may be possible."

What would happen if today you didn't think of anything pertaining to the future? Not tomorrow, not a week from now, not a year or ten years. Anything that is not happening right now you didn't focus your attention, words, thoughts or actions on. You may see that carrying these thoughts, attentions and actions weighs you down today. Does it not? So, if you were to die tomorrow, if you were told you would not live past tomorrow, would you worry about two days from now, a week from now, five years from now? Would getting that job matter? Would making sure the house is spotless matter? Would being angry about something that happened yesterday matter anymore? Would achieving that promotion or degree matter now? Would holding on to hurt from ten years ago really matter at this juncture?

There are always questions to be asked. In questions we find answers. Giving yourself a question and pondering it will naturally bring forth an answer. Now, deciphering if it is the best answer that will lead you on your higher path is another thing. Our internal self or soul knows all the true answers or the best decisions in any circumstance. It is the mind that deceives us and gives us false answers. Then we make decisions that are not in our best interest. When faced with a decision to make, here is a good question to ask: If I were completely content and happy in this moment with just myself and nothing more, and I had no fear of the future, past or a desired result, what would I do? What choice would I make? Fear tricks the mind into making decisions or giving us answers that are not in our best interest. All fear is created from a past event or from the unknown. The unknown can be seen as things we can't find fact in or as the future. The future is unknown to us. We have no idea what the future holds for us. What awaits us? What doesn't await us, right? Ah, did you catch that last sentence? It is something the mind would say. That phrase is our fear talking, not our higher self. If the higher self was talking it would always see the future filled with abundance. A future filled with a plethora of wonderful, beautiful things awaiting us. To hold on to something now because you are afraid of not having it in the future causes suffering in the now and in the future. When fear is talking you usually hold on to things that aren't in your best interest or your highest good. Our attachments to people, relationships, objects or experiences are all based on fear. Are you fearful? Most of us do not want to admit to our fears. To become aware that we are fearful beings is hard to swallow. It makes us seem weak. The fact is most of us are fueled by fear in every moment of our lives. Every thought we have, the words that come from our mouth, and every action we make is fueled by some sort of fear. It can be a conscious fear that we are aware of or an unconscious fear, which is fear we are not fully aware of that is steering our ship. A common unconscious fear is fear of the future. We are afraid something may happen in the future or something may not, so then our thoughts, words and actions are an automatic result of this fear.

The only way to truly be able to see the falsity in our reality and make the best choices that are for our greatest good is to be able to connect with our higher self. The higher self will be drowned out by the mind filled with thought. Therefore, you must be able to quiet your mind to truly be able to hear the voice of the soul within. Balance your mind, body and soul and go within the space of nothingness—the space we are all afraid to go to but where the wondrous abundance of heaven resides.

The Sum of Everything

As we close on this second book, are there more questions in your mind? Are you more confused? Or do you find your mind a little more silent? Silence is good as peace can only be found in the space where there are no thoughts, no chatter. As we individually dig more into the sum of everything, which equals all that is a part of the universe, we uncover more of who we really are. The sum of all our parts is vast and eternal, therefore, we have much to learn and much to discuss. Let us forever marinate in everything of this world, that is human, everything of the cosmos, that is living, that is heaven, which is all the dimensions of time and space. You think this is too much for the human mind? This is too much for your miniscule existence in the whole of everything? I beg to differ. As you realize the immensity of the physical world and heaven you see that what you give meaning to is pointless. What is going on in the world and your current internal struggles have no meaning in the grand scheme of things. Once you realize this they disappear from your mind and heart. The world around you is just a play on the physical. A big stage where life is just one big fictional production. A story created by you. You can see it as the script which was pre-written with the ending already decided. Or you can see it more like an improvisation with no script whereby each moment can be created by you however you see fit.

So what do you want to create? Life is about where you focus your energy. To create something you must stick with it. To truly transform you must become what you desire. This could be related to improving your physical health, experiencing more bliss or changing your circumstances. Remember that a mind, body and soul in balance will mirror this in every aspect of your life, in your physical appearance, your relationships and your circumstances. Focus on creating balance within and your life will reflect it back to you.

We now leave each other here with more questions but hopefully more answers than you began the book with. That is why I promise you that there is more to come, way more to come. We cannot sum the entirety of everything up in two books. We will continue as long as your minds and hearts long for change and answers. The goal is to get you to that place where you no longer search and you no longer struggle. All humans and creatures no matter their physical confine, status, religion, culture or beliefs are seen as one. That you all realize when one struggles, you all struggle. In that awareness, you no longer search for selfish gratification but strive to better each and every living creature on your planet. Where you give you receive. This holds true for all things, humans, animals and the earth. Animals are souls like you in a different physical form. Your true mother is the ground you are walking on. She provides you with the sustenance to live, breathe and exist. Currently, you all co-exist separately not together. That is the foundation for all your current woes.

There is a person waiting for your kindness and love. There is many an experience waiting for you. There is a light inside you that the world is waiting to see. Don't waste any more time. Go now as it is the perfect time for anything and everything.

Until we meet again may you see the abundance in the world around you. May you stop just for a moment and see the truth in front of you. Let its beauty take your breath away and let the silence envelop you. This is peace, my friend. For all you've experienced and searched for, you have finally found it. Now all you have to do it sit back and let the abundance of the universe reveal itself. For it is all right in front of you.

May all of you who find this book in your hands connect back to your inner light. May you be eternally blessed by the abundance of the earth. May you experience peace, even if for a moment, and may you live your heaven on earth.

About the Author

Ahmi Beppu is the author of The Sum of Everything book series. She is a dedicated Quantum Healing Hypnosis Practitioner, Intuitive, Clairvoyant, Clairaudient and Clairsentient. Ahmi has been utilizing her spiritual gifts helping clients around the world in remembering who they really are so that they may live their heaven on earth. You can learn more about the author at www.ahmibeppu.com.

www.ingramcontent.com/pod-product-compliance
Lightning Source LLC
La Vergne TN
LVHW041211080426
835508LV00011B/910